STOLEN IDEN

Unveiling the Real John Kennedy Jr.

STOLEN IDENTITY

UNVEILING THE REAL JOHN KENNEDY JR.

JOHN F. KENNEDY JR.

YOUR STORY MEMOIRS

Book Cover by Jacqueline Goldman and David Johnson

Edition (2) 2023

This book is dedicated to my mother, father, sister, and all the Kennedys who were lost but never forgotten.

"There's a plot in this country to enslave every man, woman, and child. Before I leave this high and noble office, I intend to expose this plot."

— John F Kennedy

CONTENTS

INTRODUCTION

My name is David Keith Quigley. I did not ask for that name. It was given to me by federal agents after my father, President John F. Kennedy, was assassinated, and I was put in the witness protection program. But what people don't know is that the murders didn't stop with him.

My mother, Jacqueline Kennedy Onassis, and her husband—my stepfather, Aristotle Onassis—were murdered in 1975. My mother was replaced with a body double who wore oversized, dark sunglasses to disguise her appearance.

My sister, Caroline Kennedy, was, I believe, murdered and replaced early in her life. I can't remember seeing my real sister after she was between the ages of ten and twelve. What happened to her is a mystery and deserves its own book, but I will do my best to relate my memories of Caroline in these pages.

The man the world knew as John Kennedy Jr. was my body double. He showed up at my school when I was nine and sat next to me in class. I was John, and he was called John-John. The mafia loves nick-names like that: "Scarface," "Joe Bananas," "Jackie Nose," and "John-John." The nickname is a moniker that describes their identifying characteristic; in this case, that he was the double.

If you look at photographs of me in the White House, you will see that I have detached earlobes and a pug nose. The man who replaced me had attached earlobes and a sharp nose. And yes, he is dead. I personally saw his lifeless, bloated body after his plane crashed into the Atlantic Ocean in 1999. If someone were to appear on the public stage, declare himself to be John Kennedy Jr., and tell the world that he faked his death, that person would be another body double.

Our government is a murder crime ring whose modus operandi is identity theft. That's how the mafia works. They are like hermit crabs, crawling into the shells of their deceased fellow beings to take over their identities, launder billions of dollars, and gain total control over humanity.

All of these murders were committed to steal the fortunes of the Kennedy and Onassis families. The actions and attitudes of those who committed these heinous acts go beyond evil and greed. They exist in a world of crazy that ordinary people would struggle to comprehend. It has its own language, culture, and code of conduct. For most of my life, I was a kite in the ferocious storm of that crazy. Somehow, someone down below had a grip on the end of the string, and so I am still here, alive to tell my story.

My life has been a living hell. I have been tortured, abused, and kept in poverty to prevent me from sharing the truth. Along the way, there have been individuals and organizations, like the Hell's Angels, who risked—and sometimes gave—their lives to protect me. I will forever be grateful to my brothers, the Hell's Angels, for what they sacrificed to protect the life of the son of a murdered president. They are not the criminals Bill Clinton declared them to be, but rather a justice league, and need to be recognized as such.

I am also grateful to the rogue government agents who perceived what was happening as evil and disregarded orders, risking their lives and careers to save me. There are some good guys out there, but they are not organized. They are individuals with a soul and a conscience, which is illuminated like the strike of a match when they brush up against abhorrent happenings.

And I will forever be thankful to a man I knew only as Wayne, a protecting angel who was always present to save, shield, and guide me through the awful reality of my life. I never knew precisely who Wayne was, except that he was a powerful man with connections to the highest levels of government, the entertainment industry, and the underworld.

Once, when an agent asked Wayne how to cause someone to forget things, he replied, "Torture." I have been tortured many times, and as a result, there are gaps in my memory, and it is difficult for me to remember names and dates. There was also the total confusion of being ferried between lives with the Kennedys, the Quigleys, The Hell's Angels, and many other locations around the world where I was sent for periods of time. I am, therefore, presenting my story as best I can as anecdotes, episodes, and short narratives, each about a different time in my life.

Sometimes, people ask me, "If you're JFK, how could you still be alive?" As if to imply that I'm lying or perhaps suggest that they wished I were. That hurts my feelings because I think, "Thank God I am!" It is essential that I live long enough to tell this story because our country is in danger, and it terrifies me. It should terrify you. By the time you reach the end of this book, you will understand, and once you understand, you must act. Don't sit back. Don't trust the plan. The plan is not for your well-being.

BOOK ONE

LOSS, ABUSE, AND MK-ULTRA

SHATTERED INNOCENCE

I have only a few memories of that time in American history that shine like a buried moon in the mind of every citizen. I was born two weeks after my father, John Fitzgerald Kennedy was elected president, and I was three years old when he was murdered. This is what I remember from those early years.

I remember colors. I remember sitting in a red upholstered sports car and being so taken by the color! I remember being on a golf course and my father walking ahead of me. My focus was on the grass, which was so green! All I could think was, "Wow, look at this grass!"

I remember watching my father getting ready to give a speech and being captivated by a woman with a wand-like device steaming the wrinkles out of his suit. The next thing I knew, he was gone, and I ran around looking for him. When I found him, he was in the middle of giving his speech.

And I recall being with him in a car, just the two of us. He was frustrated and upset and pounded the steering wheel as he reprimanded himself.

He said, "Oh shit, they're going to kill me. They are absolutely going to kill me."

But when we got out of the car, there were people there, and he was as calm as day.

The day my father was shot, I was in my bedroom at the White House. I remember the toys on the floor and the colorful pictures on the walls. Some secret service agents entered and told me my father was dead.

I looked at them, confused. *Dead? What's dead?*

After that, they had me practice saluting over and over. I did that for hours. On the day of the funeral, Bobby Kennedy stood behind me and gave me a little nudge, the prearranged signal for me to step forward and salute as my father's coffin passed.

The secret service agents also told me to pick out my favorite toy to put on my father's casket at the funeral. I got my toy airplane on a string and brought it with me. But on the day of the funeral, they took it away and handed me a PT 109 boat, a model of the one my father was on when a Japanese Destroyer struck it during World War II.

They put my plane on the ground, or someone stole it, but I couldn't find it afterward. I felt upset about that, but then I was distracted by a man dressed in a colorful kilt with bagpipes and adorned with shiny medals. I thought he was a clown and asked my mother if I could go over to him.

That's all I remember from that day.

My memories of life after my father's death are scattered leaves. They are the fallouts of multiple explosions. I will try to relate them to you in the following pages. As you read, I believe you will understand why it was difficult for me to formulate a cohesive timeline and know my age when particular events happened. Much of that is related to the fact that I was a victim of MK-Ultra, known then as Project Artichoke. I often did not know how I got to a particular place and felt restricted in terms of what I could say or ask. I refer to these experiences as "being under."

Another factor that adds to my confusion is that, after being placed in witness protection, I was given a new birthday, six years younger than my actual age, a new name, and was even made to stop being left-handed. The Quigleys, my new family, bleached my hair and had me take a cocktail of hormone pills every morning. The torture and evil I experienced while in their care shattered my mind and stole my innocence. I went from being loved and protected to being assaulted and abused as quickly as the bang from a burst balloon.

QUIGLEY LIFE

All I remember from ages three to five is flying around the world and staying at different places for periods. Some of the people were nice, and some were not so nice. Some of them seemed worried that I was even there.

Then, when I was five, I was dropped off at what looked like an old, two-story white house that had been converted into a school. Downstairs, there were classrooms, and I remember having to sign my name in a register. Upstairs were more rooms, and one of them had a bed. They told me it was my room and I should sleep. Then, after I fell asleep, a creepy man came in, pulled down my pajamas, and raped me. I felt a burning, stabbing pain and wept.

Afterward, he slapped me on the back of my head for getting blood on his genitals and told me to shut up and never say a word about it. But when I was picked up by a couple whose names I don't recall, I said, "My butt hurts. It really hurts."

The man said, "Forget it, kid. That's the way it goes."

The woman gasped and said with alarm, "I'm not going for this. This is nonsense."

He raised a shoulder, shook his head dismissively, and told her, "That's how it is. That's how we teach them."

His chilling words swirled around me like stinging hail pellets, but I understood that the woman was appalled and wanted to protect me.

Before I entered the witness protection program, I was about five years old, sitting on the cream-carpeted floor of a living room, idly rolling a truck back and forth as some adults chatted. My ears perked up when I heard my name.

They were talking about owning me, buying and selling me. On one side of the coffee table, there were Kennedys, but I didn't know who the other people were.

After that conversation, Wayne strode into the room. Short, muscular, and bullish but with a distinctive Kennedy bearing, Wayne emanated power and intelligence.

He lifted his chin and said to them, "You own this kid?"

A man nodded and said, "Yeah, I own him."

And Wayne said, "Well, I want to buy him from you."

I will always remember that. Own me? What did that mean? How can you own someone? I didn't understand it, but after that day, Wayne was a constant in my life.

He had a particular interest in me, and I remember that at the age of ten, he brought me to a cereal factory in Pennsylvania owned by the Kennedy family. Inside were old brick buildings with a train track running through the middle of the complex. They had recently done some landscaping, covering the ground of a rest area encircled by benches with white pebbles. As we sat on a bench looking around, Wayne picked up a small black rock and tossed it into the middle of the white ones.

Turning to me, he said, "That's you. You're that black rock. You stand out from everybody."

At age five, I was made to live with a family named Quigley. They lived in a large ranch house with a big yard, a chicken coop, horses, and a hog pen in Clovis, California. That's when the government changed my name to David Keith Quigley.

From this point on, my memories are like broken fragments of smashed china. So many traumatic things happened that broke my mind. My life was divided between my time with the Quigleys; sojourns with my mother, Jackie, to different locations around the world; time spent in New York City, where I attended school on and off; life on the Greek Island of Skorpios, and the yacht, "The Christina" with the Onassis'; and journeys and Black Ops with Wayne.

These are the shards of memories of my time with the Quigleys. They can be assembled as a mosaic to form an image of what it was like to live there.

Max Quigley was a big, square man with thin dark hair who looked like an extra in a cowboy western. Dorothy was more Irish-looking, with blue eyes and curly red hair. Her usual blank expression hid a dark and poisonous personality. Max and Dorothy had three children: Max Jr., Richard, and Deborah. Anyone would take them for a typical, church-going family. No one would guess the truth: that they were involved in organized crime, child trafficking, and kidnapping.

I remember being around five years old, and my new brother Richard said he was going to visit his friend Nathan, who lived down the street. I wanted to come along, so I ran after him. When we got to Nathan's, they tied me to a lamppost by my arms and feet and left me hanging there for a long time, crying and screaming. Finally, Max and Dorothy showed up to untie me. Then, when we got home, Dorothy took me into my bedroom and beat me with a two-by-four for allowing myself to get tied to a lamppost by my brother.

In the early days, the Quigleys managed a restaurant, but they were fired for stealing, so Max went to work at a poultry farm. Not long after that, Max stopped feeding the hogs for a few days, starving them for when the bodies showed up. I don't know who they were—possibly the people who fired them—but the hogs devoured them in minutes. There was nothing left.

That week, my new grandmother, Marie Quigley, showed me how to kill a chicken when she chopped its head off on a butcher block in the backyard. Though its head was gone, it ran off, splattering blood in a broken, jagged line across the newly painted white fence.

Every morning, I was made to take a handful of pills with breakfast. The Quigleys told me it was a vitamin regime, but I suspect they were hormone pills to keep me looking younger. For years, I didn't have a birthday. I was just a little kid and had to watch my new siblings have birthday celebrations every year, but there was never one for me.

After some years, they gave me a new birthdate: January 15, 1966, six years younger than my actual age. It wasn't difficult to pull off this deception. I was away from home so often and missed so much school that no one really knew me. When I was home, if I didn't want to go to school, Dorothy didn't care. She let me stay home and watch TV. Also, we lived in a closed community, and everyone was either a member of or connected to the same secret society. Crazy happenings were part of everyday life.

The Quigleys also did everything they could to disguise my identity, including putting lemon juice in my hair and making me stand out in the sun to lighten it. I was left-handed as a child, but even that could have been an identifying characteristic, so every time I put out my left hand to reach for something, Max or Dorothy slapped it. Finally, I learned to use my right hand.

Occasionally, the Quigleys brought me to public places where Jackie or other family members could see me but not speak to me to ensure my safety. Once, we were at Barnum and Bailey's Circus, and Jackie was seated a few places down from us. Another time, they took me to a Denny's restaurant, and she was sitting with some people a few booths away. I wanted to approach her, but the Quigleys told me, "Just shut up and eat your food, kid."

After a few years in Cisco, we moved to Fresno and finally settled in the community of Yosemite Lakes in Coarsegold, California. This, too, was a closed community consisting of ranch houses spread out from one another at considerable distances. All the families had the Masonic Bible in their homes and were members of secret societies.

In the middle of the night, they used to put up a tent on the grounds of somebody's thousand-acre ranch and conduct masonic rituals. We were told to refer to one another as 'brother' and 'sister,' perhaps to give us the sense that we were all part of the same family, and possibly so that, in later years, we wouldn't remember each other's names.

As children, they taught us how to make tea lights for these backyard rituals. That's where you poke holes with a can opener around the side of a can and put a candle in it. That way, the light only shines down when you hang it up. Even an aircraft flying overhead wouldn't be able to see anything. We would attend these meetings as young kids, and someone would preach: "Your job is to go kill, steal, and bring me money."

A girl I was close to told me she was gang-raped at one of those ceremonies. Terrible things happened there. I was present for some of them.

I remember being dragged out in the middle of the night and put on a stump under a tree with a noose around my neck. Someone kicked the stump out, and I thought I would die, but the rope wasn't tied to the tree. Other times, they had me lie on a table, and they got out a ceremonial knife. All the adults would take turns walking by, acting like they were going to stab me. During these rituals, there was always someone there to make sure no one went crazy and actually did it, but incidents like that messed with my mind.

Another time, they took me to the graveyard, made me pull up weeds, and told me those were my parents' graves, and I killed them.

I also remember a frightening incident from when I was very young, and the Quigleys had a child in the house. I was in my room and couldn't stop crying because I could hear them doing something terrible to this child. Dorothy came in and beat me, which just made me cry more.

The next day, Max took something out in a trash bag. To this day, I don't know what happened, but I remember Dorothy used to buy vaporizers. I learned that spraying mist in the air helps a person see the spirit leave the body when someone dies. These people would try and capture that. It gave them power, somehow. I don't know how.

Once, the Quigleys brought over two little girls under five years old and casually said, "These are your cousins." They introduced them as Heidi and Jeanette, claiming they were Dorothy's brother Richard Crisp's children. But I had never seen them before; they popped out of nowhere.

I recall once when we were at their place, I was pushing them around in a wheelbarrow. Looking back, it's clear that those kids were victims of child kidnapping and trafficking, but they appeared unaware of what was happening and didn't grasp that they wouldn't return home.

Years later, in the '90s, Richard's ex-wife Anita broke down and cried before me, saying, "I'm so, so sorry they've done this to you!"

What struck me about Anita was that she looked so much like my mother, Jackie, and I wondered if she had played the part of one of Jackie's doubles.

Once, I met John Gotti getting off a plane that had just landed on a dirt runway near a cow field in O'Niel, California. Those guys flew back and forth all the time. They liked to have sex with lots of women and get them pregnant to have a big family.

He flew in one night when I and a bunch of other kids were gathered in a big tent for a worship ceremony. Gotti was talking about going to some girl's house and screwing her. I knew this girl. She was living with handlers, like me and the Quigleys.

I said, "You're not going to screw my sister in the middle of the night!"

The guy with him shoved me on the ground and said, "You need to show this man a little respect."

Years later, I couldn't believe it when an HBO special made John Gotti look like some hero. He was responsible for the deaths of hundreds of people, and the only reason he was the 'Teflon Don,' where charges never stuck, was because he was also a government agent. But in the end, I guess he went too far, and his family gave him up.

A point of confusion is where organized crime ends and the government begins. What is above them? I don't have the answers to all these questions. I wish I did, but I can only present my knowledge and experiences. Our government is an organized crime unit; organized crime families like the mafia are connected to the government. Secret societies, child trafficking, and human sacrifice rituals are all a part of—and connected to—this nefarious jigsaw puzzle of *The Garden of Hell.*

My world was so crazy and confusing that I could never make sense of it. People wanted to kill me, yet they couldn't, somehow. You could call it Divine intervention or a combination of seen and unseen forces, but I can't even count the number of attempts made on my life.

For example, I rode motorbikes my whole life. I even rode my bike two miles to the bus stop when I went to school. One day, I was driving my motorbike down a dirt road and coming up on a bend where the road snaked around a river. I tried my brakes, but they didn't work, so I started down-shifting, almost crashing into a tree in front of the river.

But the tree didn't kill me, and I didn't end up in the river. Somehow, I managed to turn up on the road where a house was on the corner. I saw my friend, a high schooler who lived there, and a younger kid standing in the front yard, laughing at me. I looked at them, shocked, then got off my bike to check the brakes and saw they had been loosened.

"It was just a funny joke," one shouted through cupped palms.

My heart still pounded like crazy from the close call, and I said, "I thought you guys were my friends!"

They could have killed me. They very nearly did. But shortly after that, the older kid who loosened the brakes joined the military. I asked about him and was told that somehow when he was in training, he fell out of a helicopter to his death.

Max and Dorothy Quigley were crooks through and through. As a youngster, I went stream fishing with Max up the hills near Shaver Lake at a place called Dinkey Creek. On the way, we would stop off at an old sawmill. Bikers would pull up, and Max would give them a paper shopping bag. I was curious the first time that happened and went over to see what was in there. Before Max could stop me, I saw the plastic sacks filled with white powder, like confectioner's sugar.

Max was also a counterfeiter and printed hundred-dollar bills on a counterfeiting machine in the attic. I remember watching the bills tossed around in the dryer with poker chips so the bits of color would rub off on them and make them look more authentic. Once, we went on a road trip and were violently ill after getting a meal at A&W; only we couldn't go back and complain since we'd paid with a counterfeit hundred.

Presidential books and commemorative magazines often contain codes for clued-in readers to interpret. An example is a photograph and accompanying caption featured in the JFK. Jr. commemorative issue of Life Magazine in 1999: *John F. Kennedy Jr. An album of unseen and unforgettable pictures.* It includes an allusion to Max Quigley and his counterfeit hundreds, probably a source of ridicule within the mafia.

Nestled between a collection of artistic, professional photographs is an obscure, blurry picture taken in Greece by an unseen photographer with a telephoto lens. It is of Aristotle, John-John, and an "unidentified friend" (me). The caption beneath is bizarre and cryptic, stating that *Ari could be very generous and, on one occasion, gave John two crisp, hundred dollar bills to buy fishing bait.*

Decoded, that message could be interpreted as follows: "Crisp" refers to the Crisp family. (Dorothy's maiden name was Crisp, and the message implies that the boy in the photo was hiding with them.) Max counterfeited hundred dollar bills if the knowledgeable reader wanted to know which Crisp family member was being referred to. "Fishing bait" means "bait and switch." In other words, the two boys in the photograph had their identities switched.

From Life Magazine: Me, John-John, and Ari in Greece. The cap-tion reads: "...on another occasion (Onassis) handed over two crisp 100 dollar bills to buy bait for a fishing trip."

Dorothy got her real estate license and was as crooked as they come. She got involved in a scheme to flip properties after getting them falsely appraised for a higher price than they were worth. Then, she helped buyers get falsified income records to get mortgages on the land they purchased at the inflated price.

Before she went to trial, the Quigleys paid someone to be her body double. A fake Dorothy Quigley was convicted and sentenced to prison. Then, they got rid of the double before she was scheduled to serve her sentence.

The attempts on my life by the Quigleys started in earnest after Dorothy's sister, Opal May Edwards, promised me her fortune. Despite her wealth, Opal May was an eccentric millionaire and had quirky habits, probably due to living through the Depression. She saved rubber bands and aluminum foil and didn't trust banks. One time, she bought me a pickup truck that cost 1,200 dollars, and when she went to pay for it, she just popped open the glove compartment box and took out a stack of hundreds.

Shortly after her husband Daryl died, I found myself in the Quigley's garage with Opal May. I always suspected Daryl's involvement in my father's death. (The Mafia made you rich if you had anything to do with the Kennedy assassination.) While tinkering with my bike, Opal May leaned against a work table, pursed her lips, and spoke to me in a voice full of purpose.

She said, "I want you to remember my name. There's some funny business going on here. My name is Opal May Edwards. I left you enough so you'll never have to worry about money again. And if you ever have a child, your child will never have to worry about money. Please, remember my name."

Opal May disappeared after that. I never saw her again, or her money either. But the Quigleys got wind of the whole thing, and after that, they tried to kill me over and over again. Years later, I tracked down her grave in Colorado and talked to the groundskeeper there. He said he remembered that funeral well because no one showed up. That didn't sound right to me. Dorothy Quigley would not have missed her sister's funeral.

I never had the money to pursue an investigation, so I remained in the dark about Opal May's fate and the millions of dollars she left behind. I know Max Quigley used to try and forge papers in her name, and it's possible the body in that grave in Colorado is not Opal May, but I'll never know for sure.

Once, I asked Wayne about it and if he thought I would ever see that money.

He shook his head decisively and said, "That book is closed."

Confused, I asked, "What book?"

Wayne clenched his jaw in frustration and said angrily, "Those Quigleys didn't teach you shit! I paid them all that money to teach you."

I thought the book reference must be related to something I often witnessed during the peculiar ceremonies in the middle of the night. Under a big tent, they'd take out a giant-sized book, and a designated writer would record the narrative they were crafting, detailing their plan. They would make up a story of what they were going to do and how they would do it. The written scenarios were like blueprints for how these plans would be executed. For example, they might pick out someone who's a billionaire, like Donald Trump, and they'd create a scenario in a book about how they would steal his money. Then, they would carry out that plan.

Another thing that happened at these big family meetings was that we would be made to look at a movie screen while names of prominent people—some dead—would scroll like credits. We were forbidden to speak the names of people who had passed. Also at these meetings, if somebody made a negative comment or a clever remark, someone else would grab them, whisk them off, and they'd never be seen again.

I don't know if Wayne knew how the Quigleys were treating me, but I do remember once, during winter, Max and Dorothy were visibly nervous, muttering things like, "They're going to kill us."

I was just a little kid then, but they dropped me off at a Big Bear, California church camp. Snow was on the ground, and a stream ran through the middle of the campgrounds. While I was there, camp counselors taught me how to do trick riding on a horse. They took pictures of me doing things like standing up on the saddle, and I felt like they knew I was John Kennedy Jr., and they were documenting all this for some purpose.

They also had me do something called "the polar bear," where I dove into icy water and held onto a rock while they timed me to see how long I could hold my breath underwater.

The Quigleys were also meant to be camping there, but they changed their plans at the last minute. On visiting days, they never showed up. I sat at a picnic table by myself and waited, but no one came.

In the 1970s, people were hearing about chip implants for pets so that they could locate their lost animals. However, the capabilities of these chips far exceeded what the public was told, and the technology had existed much longer. Those chips weren't just implanted in pets, either.

Around the age of ten, the Quigleys took me on a cross-country journey to a naval base near Mechanicsburg, Pennsylvania. This base included a once lavish two-story hotel and spa frequented by the wealthy in the 1800s, who came to take mineral baths. During World War II, it was repurposed by the navy into a manufacturing plant, and by the 1970s, it was pretty rundown.

Max and Dorothy dropped me off there, and I was taken upstairs to a room converted into a doctor's office. In the room, a nurse, who looked to be in her fifties, and an eerie-looking doctor, likely in his seventies, were waiting for me. The nurse instructed me to sit in a chair similar to a dentist's, and they shaved off a section of my hair.

I heard a whirring sound and felt some pressure but no pain. They carefully cut a small, round disc from my skull and placed it beside me on a stainless steel tray. Seeing a perfect circle of my skull left me completely shocked. After some procedure, they delicately reinserted the cut piece back into my head and bandaged it.

Then they attached wires to my head and showed me a picture of a boy who had been kidnapped. The doctor told me to "use my third eye" to find this kid. Images of blood, gore, and body parts flooded my mind. I screamed and ripped the wires off.

"What are you doing to me?" I yelled.

They ignored me, wrapped a cloth bandage around my head, and then the nurse brought me downstairs. All the way back to California, I wore that rag around my head and fought back images of hacked-up body parts.

Following that incident, I found myself entangled in the world of MK-Ultra and Project Artichoke. These experiences included instances of lost time, nocturnal abductions to various locations, and surreal occurrences. I will describe a few of these experiences and why they are significant.

My Odyssey Through MK-Ultra

M K-Ultra is a technique government agents use to control people's minds through torture and hypnosis. In my day, it was called Project Artichoke, and Wayne told me never to speak of it. However, since then, most information about the project has been made public, and I feel it's essential to share some of my experiences in the program.

To the best of my understanding, the chip I received at the military base in Pennsylvania serves two purposes: It functions as a GPS locator so federal agents can always track my whereabouts, and it also works as a mind control device. The people in control of this project used certain code words or trigger phrases, similar to what a hypnotist does, to cause me to remember or forget an experience.

As a mind-control device, the chip worked because after I went to sleep, some signal was sent via a remote control. Then, either

Wayne or federal agents would enter my room, wake me up, and from that point on, I operated in a trance-like state.

It's difficult to explain what it feels like to be in this state except to say it's like being partially asleep yet still conscious and aware. During this period, anyone who might speak or interact with me would have no idea that I was "under."

Mostly, I don't remember being taken, except once, when I was conscious in a car, and an agent who was driving said, "You need to start paying attention to where we're going. Look at the street signs. Notice where we are."

He spoke as if this were one of our many conversations, driving God knows where in the middle of the night. But that's the only time I remember speaking to him.

Most of the time, Wayne took me places, and I can recall being there and what happened, but I have no idea what our location was or how we got there. When Wayne wanted me to remember, he probably used the trigger phrases I'd been programmed with before putting me back to bed.

It's possible that I lived entire weeks or even months in an MK-altered state without anyone knowing. I believe I was under MK control much of the time I spent in New York, attending school and living with Jackie. I have very few memories of being there, but thousands of photographs attest to my life in New York as a child, attending St. David's and later the Collegiate School.

The first time I noticed something strange was going on was when a friend came over when I was at the Quigleys and said, "Where have you been?"

I looked at him, confused, and said, "What do you mean, where have I been? I was just over at your house yesterday."

He narrowed his eyes at me and said, "What the hell are you talking about? That was two weeks ago!"

Another time, I ran across a schoolmate, and he said, "What were the ambulance and sheriff doing over at your house yesterday?"

I said, "What are you talking about? There was no ambulance or police."

His jaw dropped, and he said, "You really don't remember? There were police and an ambulance. It was a big deal."

But I didn't understand what he was talking about. I could have sworn I was home that day.

I remember some things, but I know there are plenty more that I don't. I've found that the best time to try and remember is when I'm relaxed, almost like I'm about to fall asleep. I did that once and started counting all the murders I'd witnessed while under MK-Ultra. I got up to eighty; then I realized I was counting the same ones over again.

Sometimes, with MK-Ultra, what you're witnessing is so horrific that you wake up from the trance state. I remember being locked in a bathroom with a dead body in the bathtub. My abductors wouldn't let me out until I chopped the body into small pieces.

Another time, they were torturing someone in a 55-gallon drum of water. (At least, I believe it was water.) Something about it horrified me, and I started to wake up and fight them. They grabbed

JOHN F. KENNEDY JR.

me, put me in a chair, and stuck bamboo under my fingernails as punishment for waking up or as a way of torturing me so that I would block the whole thing out and not remember.

I once saw a little boy stomped to death by a horse. I knew the family. The father was a judge named Burton, and I went to school with the Burton kids.

One day, Victor, a federal agent who lived in my neighborhood and was friends with Max Jr., took me to their house. They had drugged me, and I was coming out of it, but I had a migraine headache and couldn't get out of the car, so I saw the whole thing from the car window.

There were probably eight or nine men there. They were holding onto the judge and his youngest child, a boy. Then they got the family horse, threw the kid on the ground, and purposely made the horse trample him to death.

It was such a tight-knit community in Coarsegold that I knew one of the guys who did it and his wife and daughter. The papers wrote the whole thing up like the boy was killed in an accident with his horse, but it was murder, probably in retribution for a court ruling or as a threat for an upcoming trial: *Make the ruling in our favor, or we'll kill someone else from your family.*

MK-Ultra involves a lot of torture. Torture makes you forget, and it fractures your mind. People talk about waterboarding, but that's child's play compared to the stuff our government has. I remember being put in a contraption that looked like the cockpit of an airplane. I don't know where I was—possibly Guantanamo. (They've got some crazy shit going on at Guantanamo.) But they lowered the plexiglass hood over me, and initially, I heard a sequence of numbers, something like 3,8,4,6,1,2...Then, I got slammed with the most excruciating pain I ever felt. I couldn't stop screaming, and all the while, the mechanical voice was repeating the same sequence of numbers.

When it stopped, I was so exhausted from screaming at the top of my lungs that I collapsed. Someone lifted the lid, and despite being relieved it was over, I was unable to move or get up.

That experience happened when I was a kid, but I experienced something similar in my twenties. They placed me in a soundproof room, and an ear-piercing noise filled the space. It was so loud I thought I would go deaf. I screamed, covered my ears, and sank to my knees.

Around the same age, I woke up thinking I'd had a crazy dream about making cement. In the "dream," the people I was with had just killed a woman, and my job was to mix cement in a cement mixer so they could bury her in a basement.

The thing with cement is it gets your hands really chapped. The next day, I woke up in my truck and looked at my hands. They were all chapped with cement residue, and my shirt smelled like kerosene. So, it hadn't been a dream, but the surreal nature of these experiences often blurs the line between reality and a nightmare.

I've seen MK-Ultra done to other people as well. One incident that stands out occurred in Illinois in my twenties. A guy from one of the families tried to run me over in his Corvette. He was considered a bad seed within the mafia. So they got him under MK and put him in his car. We drove down the road and passed a rest stop with trucks neatly lined up in a parking area.

Before we got out of the car, Wayne leaned over to the guy and said, "Here's what you're going to do, Buddy. You're going to go 150 miles an hour down the side of the road, and don't stop. Just keep going."

So the guy sped down the side of the road at 150 miles an hour and ended up decapitating beneath the first massive truck parked there. I have to admit that one didn't hurt my feelings too badly.

THE PLAN DEBUNKED

Wayne often took me while I was under MK-Ultra to witness certain events, and although I didn't understand why then, I knew he wanted me to remember these moments and understand the true nature of specific individuals. I believe it was all meant for this time in 2023 because these experiences hold relevance today. It might sound unbelievable, but Illuminati families plan decades ahead, and their plans involve thwarting the awakening of humanity, which was meant to happen now in the 21st century. The Illuminati, therefore, orchestrated a false awakening called simply "Q."

Family members had to silence me to ensure the awakening was steered in their favor. They were desperate to do so, even though their future-looking technology told them their goals were unwinnable. What can I tell you? They are insane, but they did everything to prevent my information from coming out.

Some tried to block my story by keeping me on the run and in poverty or else by trying to kill me, but they failed. Others—good guys who knew this day was coming and secretly looked forward to it—did what they could to ensure evidence would exist to support my claims. Many of these positive characters were born into Illuminati families and had no choice. (Once you're in, there's no way out except through taking a dirt nap.) However, after a certain age, they seem to choose how good or bad they want to be. Some secretly aided me, but they had to be discreet and crafty.

The next photograph shows how some family members found a way to plant the evidence I would need someday. It was taken at a party, possibly a birthday celebration, where we were required to wear name tags. I thought that was silly and kept removing mine, but someone always insisted I put it back. Eventually, a photographer asked me to put it back on and then took a photograph.

Reflecting on this event, it was a way to provide photographic evidence that I was replaced. They were saying, "This is the real John Kennedy, the one with the distinctive big ears, detached lobes, and a pug nose. This is how he writes his name." And yes, I write my name, John Kennedy, precisely the same way today as it appears on that nametag.

JOHN F. KENNEDY JR.

I was used in MK for several purposes. The first reason was that Wayne wanted me to witness and remember certain events so that I could write this testimony. They all pertain to the nefarious Q-Plan, which brainwashes its followers not to do anything when they see disturbing events unfold.

"Q-Anons," as they call themselves, believe they need not act and should "trust the plan" because a secretive group of military agents called "white hats" are working to subvert the plans of the enemy, and therefore, they need not fear. Alarming government overreach should not be an indication of a pending communist takeover. Instead, "Anons" are encouraged to believe that such activity is "just a movie."

According to "The Plan," rather than panic when nefarious events appear to unfold, Q followers should rejoice because, as per the cryptic Q-Clock decodes, this means that peace, prosperity, and health (thanks to a benevolent group of aliens who gifted humanity with a miraculous healing technique called "med-beds") are about to be unveiled.

The crashing of the economy, civic unrest, and the threats of a civil or world war are all reasons to get excited because it means that their salvation, courtesy of Donald Trump and JFK Jr. (who they believe faked his death), is coming to save the day. But Donald Trump died and was replaced in 1989, and John-John died in 1999. Let me tell you about it.

The Death of Donald Trump

Wayne wanted me to one day be able to share that the real Donald Trump died in a helicopter crash in 1989. He took me to witness this event. Despite being under MK-Ultra, I vividly recall being at the crash site on the Garden State Parkway near Atlantic City, New Jersey. I can confidently say that Donald Trump perished in that crash, and Wayne meant for me to witness it.

Atlantic City was a pet project of Wayne's, and I believe he had it in his mind that I'd run the place one day. I remember when he brought me there some years after it was built up. We walked up and down the boardwalk, and he told me he owned the whole place, from the vendors on the boardwalk to the casinos.

Donald Trump was family and was put in place to run the casinos with some other mafia tycoons. But Trump and his partners must have done something to piss the family off because they were killed in that helicopter crash which was made to look like an accident.

Wayne wanted me to see it, to know that Trump was dead. When we arrived, they were pulling the bodies out of the plane and onto stretchers. The last body they pulled off was Donald Trump, and Wayne pointed at him and said, "Look."

Trump was a helicopter pilot and had been flying the chopper when the rotor blew off, and they crashed onto the Garden State Parkway. The papers reported that only three executives died in that crash, but I know Trump died, too. He was replaced with a body double who probably couldn't fly a helicopter to save his life. The real Trump would never let himself be chauffeured around in a helicopter as his double does today.

People must understand that the person who replaced Trump and ran the country for four years is a criminal, possibly a Russian spy. The Russians paid Melania to marry Trump because they knew that having a good-looking wife would boost his image and increase his chances of winning the presidency.

That's another thing Wayne brought me to see. It was on a private plane. Melania sat at a table, and in front of her was a suitcase overflowing with jewels.

She looked at it and said, "It's not enough. It's not enough for me to marry that cocksucker."

In 2016, Wayne brought me to the White House while I was "under." All he had to do was flash his badge, and we got in to see then-President Donald Trump.

I said, "I'm the real John Kennedy Junior! No one will even recognize the fact that I exist. I could kill somebody in broad daylight and get away with it."

Trump told me to "get a fucking lawyer." Then, later that week, he paraphrased what I said at a rally, announcing to the crowd: "I could stand in the middle of 5th Avenue and shoot somebody, and I wouldn't lose voters."

That comment earned him a lot of backlash from the media, as he must have known it would, but he made a point of saying it, anyway. It's crazy how, my whole life, they've kept me poor and down and out while they live lives of wealth and privilege. Yet I've seen how, time and time again, my existence plays so prominently in their psyches.

It reminds me of what Wayne said about the book on Opal May being "closed." I think the book on the real John Kennedy Jr. is still very much open, and many people know more about me than I do about myself.

The Death of John-John

I attended St. David's School in New York City on and off from age six. My memories of being there are sporadic. In my mind, I wasn't in attendance for more than a few weeks each year. However, it is possible that I was there in an MK-Ultra trance state for extended periods. I do recall that it was there that John-John, my double, first appeared in my class and sat beside me.

As mentioned, he was called "John-John" because he was a double. However, he didn't like the name, and whenever anyone called him by it, he spit in their face. I'm not exactly sure where he came from, but as we got older, Jackie and Aristotle referred to him occasionally as my brother. By that point, I was so messed up I didn't know what to think. But now it occurs to me that John-John could have been the son of Aristotle and his mistress, making him my step-brother. Whatever the case, he must have been a very conflicted child. I remember one day, he punched me in the face for no reason.

Everything was photo ops in those early years after my father's murder, and below is a famous photograph of the two of us with some other kids on an outing to an amusement park. I remember that day. The Secret Service made me wear my father's size 12 shoes, and they were so big and uncomfortable that I had to sit down and watch while the other kids ran around, went on rides, and had fun.

They also had us pick up a Black kid on the way there for publicity because it was during the civil rights struggle. That boy's name was Denzel Washington, and I remember him saying, "Yeah, they're going to make me a star. They're going to make me big in Hollywood." And I said, "Oh, that's cool."

In the picture, John-John is showing me the ring he got from John Gotti, and I am telling him about my ring, which I got from the Queen of England. John-John got his ring for committing murder when he was nine. That's the way the mob works. They lure kids into committing murder and film them. After that, they have them for life. You play along, or you go down for murder. After John-John replaced me, he became the man everyone knew as John Kennedy Jr.

My guess as to how they made the switch was that after I left, the kids stopped calling him John-John, and he became just "John." Then, the following year, they kept the same boys in each of the two classes, except for him. Since he had never been in their class, and they only knew him as John, he could easily start the next grade as John Kennedy Jr. This is a guess. I don't pretend to understand the ins and outs of these complex schemings; However, I have two more photographs that show John and I together.

At Palisades Amusement Park, May 5, 1969

The photograph below shows the two of us in the sixth grade at the Collegiate school in New York. We were learning about World War II, Nazis, and Hitler, whom the boys in the back seemed, disturbingly, to admire. John-John is fourth from the right, with his tongue sticking out, and I am third in from the left, with my hair tinted blonde, thanks to the Quigleys dousing it with lemon juice. My expression bears a noticeable MK-Ultra glaze.

Class photo from 6th grade, Collegiate School

The following photograph was taken when John-John and I were in our late teens or early twenties. I was, again, under MK and don't recall the details other than that we were doing volunteer work, and to the best of my recollection, it was in Bullhead City. (However, a newspaper article states that it was taken in Rabinal, Guatemala.) I had been moving bricks for three days and had almost finished the job when John-John arrived, and I said, "Oh, so now you get here!"

A news photographer took our picture, which appeared in the town's newspaper. I snapped a picture of us in the paper and have had it on my phone for years. A friend found it in a book where it says that the other boy is my cousin, Timothy Shriver. Timothy Shriver wasn't there that day or the two days before that. I worked my ass off, and it's me in that photo.

JFK and John-John, late '70's.

For Comparison: The photo on the left is taken from an old ID card - one of the few pictures I have of myself.

I saw John-John and Caroline's replacements on and off over the years. I had the impression my replacement was losing favor with Wayne. We were in our early 30s, and I bumped into John-John at a party. My cousin Adam was there, and the three of us were talking. John-John said he wanted to be John Gotti.

I said, "Yeah, you want to be the next John Gotti and run New York?"

He nodded and looked at me with a serious and determined gleam.

"Yeah," he said.

I don't know what John-John was doing at that point. He pissed off the mob. I started hearing crazy stories about him, similar to the newspaper story about him falling out of his kayak, swimming to shore, and breaking into someone's house. But I also heard there was more to that story than what was reported, and there had been some coverup. Basically, John-John was losing it.

A year or so after that, Wayne brought me to John-John's apartment building in New York City—a converted warehouse in Tribeca. We stood out front and waited until he coasted up to us on his bicycle. When he saw us, his face collapsed like a punctured tire.

Wayne said, "Are you going to give this guy some money? He's the real John Kennedy."

John said, "I've given all my money to the mafia. I've already paid them all. I don't have anything to give him."

As he wheeled his bicycle past us and into his building, I sensed the storm of panic brewing beneath the cool facade.

I know the whole incident wasn't about money. Wayne wasn't like that. The point was to confront John-John and scare the shit out of him. John-John was telling Wayne that the Mafia had him by the balls, and he didn't have any money, which was probably true. I don't know what he did, but he must have pissed somebody off, and now he was a marked man. So he wanted to cash out, and he needed money.

After he started dating Carolyn, Wayne played a recording for me of the two of them chatting on a helicopter. They talked about how they wanted to kill me and take some hidden money they knew about. Carolyn said, "We'll kill Dave and take his money." Then she spoke about killing the fake Jackie, saying, "It's not really your mother."

Before he met Carolyn, John-John had political aspirations, but after that, it became all about money. He opened bank accounts all over New York and New Jersey, depositing cash. Then, word got out that Jackie had cancer. I was "under" when Wayne brought me to her Upper East Side apartment.

The three of us stood in the kitchen. The fake Jackie, whom I'd known since my mother died in 1975, leaned over the table with her hands firmly planted. She spoke in a faraway voice as she stared unseeingly at the polished wood surface.

She wasn't talking to me but said, "I believe, I really believe that the children poisoned me. That's why I'm dying."

The information blasted through the carefully arranged room like a mobster in a bar fight, and my breath caught in my throat. Wayne wanted more information from her, and they left me in the kitchen and went to the living room together, where they spoke in animated, hushed tones. I sat down, putting my palms on the table where Jackie's had been, and waited.

The next time Wayne brought me there, she was dead. I was under MK and instantly panicked. I felt like I was reliving the loss of my real mother. Jackie lay in her bed, her mouth agape. I couldn't bear that and instinctively took off my bandana, gently securing it under her chin and tying it to the top of her head. It seemed idiotic, but at that moment, I couldn't stand seeing her mouth open like that.

Jackie's boyfriend, Maurice Templelsman, burst in and accused me of killing her. I looked at him in shock. I felt like I'd been slapped and didn't understand what he was saying. Later, I realized Jackie told him John did it, and Maurice thought she meant me.

Several days after Jackie's death, the press shot footage of John-John addressing the media. To my eyes, his demeanor seemed more amused than troubled, like a psychopath getting off on the public's belief in his lies. I caught up with him a few weeks later; Wayne brought me. Once again, I was in an MK-induced state, but I understood the purpose of the meeting.

We arrived on a street corner in New York, where a limo was parked outside a restaurant. Wayne indicated the open car door and told me to get in. I got in the limo and noticed John-John and Caroline dressed up. They were waiting for John's wife, Carolyn, to leave the restaurant.

When I got in, Caroline didn't say anything. She just sat there with a little smile on her face. But when he saw me, John-John went from a calm lake to a raging storm in the blink of an eye.

I said, "I think it's time I came out as the real John Kennedy."

His cheeks flamed with anger, and he said, "Hell no, you're never coming out, you motherfucker!"

He got out of the car and started yelling at Wayne, but Wayne just stood there, steadily fixing him with a measured, unwavering gaze.

Then he said, "Your days are numbered."

John stalked off, and that was that.

The next chapter unfolded with cruel, callous greed. John-John and Carolyn auctioned off all my mother's belongings at Sotheby's Auction House. It broke my heart to see my family's legacy and possessions, including letters and artwork done by me personally, paraded in front of strangers and sold to the highest bidder. There were photographs and portraits of me and my family, books and furniture that had been my father's, my mother's paintings, and family jewels, including gifts given to her by my father, all auctioned off to strangers and gone forever. John-John, his wife, and Caroline made 35 million dollars at that auction, and none of it was theirs to sell. The bitter reality of that loss lingers to this day.

In 1999, I was hanging out in front of a truck stop, waiting for my next load. As mentioned, being chipped means that federal agents can locate me anytime. That day, John-John, my cousin Adam, and an agent approached me and asked if I wanted to join them for a wedding party in Hyannis Port.

It was obviously a setup, and I responded, "Dude, I'm not going with you."

They insisted. "Come on, you'll have fun."

They were doing their best to persuade me to go, and Wayne's voice echoed in my mind, reminding me, "You're never going to figure anything out unless you go."

Deciding that unraveling the mystery was worth the risk, I agreed. I thought, "Well, I guess I'm going to go because I want to find out what's happening."

The federal agent waved me towards his car and said, "Come on, you can just go with us."

I shrugged and got in the car with them, leaving my truck behind. Our first stop was a house where we picked up Carolyn and her sister, Lauren, before heading to John's apartment in New York. Adam left us there, and I stayed in the apartment with John, Carolyn, and Lauren.

That's when I realized that Carolyn was actually a man. The revelation surprised me, and I thought, "Oh, so he's gay?" That really shook me up; the world's most eligible bachelor was gay. But I remember being forced to do all sorts of things when I was young to try and make me gay. I assumed the same was done to him. I don't know the point of it, but homosexuality is seen as an asset in that world.

The next afternoon, we drove to an airport in New Jersey. As we approached the plane, I noticed they strategically positioned themselves between me and the terminal windows so no one could see me. Once on the plane, Carolyn leaned forward to cover the window to hide me again. I was sure, at this point, they intended to kill me at the wedding. In that scenario, no one would know what happened to me. I would vanish without a trace.

Once the plane was in the air, John-John became increasingly anxious. Everyone could feel it.

Carolyn said, "What's the matter? Why are we turning?"

John's voice rang with fear. "The plane won't steer! I can only go left."

I suggested, "Just slow down, and we'll keep going in a circle."

But they wouldn't listen to me. Amid their arguing and panic, I pulled my life preserver out from under the seat and put it on. I told Lauren to do the same. Suddenly, with an unexpected impact, we slammed into the ocean. There was no warning, just an instantaneous crash.

Struggling, I managed to open the door and pulled Lauren about 20 feet away from the sinking plane. I was treading water, trying to hold onto her, but she resisted, saying, "I have to go get my sister!"

I realized I'd have to let her go or knock her out, but she got away from me anyway and started swimming towards the sinking plane. I don't know if she made it inside or just got near it, but the plane went down fast at that point, and she went with it.

I was in the water for what seemed like an eternity, pushing down on the shoulders of my life preserver so I could see and scan the misty darkness for any sign of ship or shoreline. Hours passed, and I went into a state of shock.

I don't remember when the ship finally appeared, but I was hoisted onboard, shivering uncontrollably. Blankets were piled on me as I lay there. I recall seeing the captain pacing nervously in front of me before losing consciousness. Later, I discovered the captain's anxiety stemmed from a call from Bill Clinton ordering him to throw me back into the ocean.

I don't know how much time passed before Wayne came and picked me up from the hospital. He drove me to the warehouse where they were reconstructing the plane, scattered wreckage covering the floor. A man approached Wayne and handed him a quarter, saying, "This was found in the steering mechanism. That's what took the plane down."

Considering the imagery on the quarter, George Washington's face, it looked like a typical mob hit—George for *George Magazine*.

Wayne brought me to another section of the warehouse, and I saw John-John's swollen body, grotesquely distorted. As with Donald Trump, I know that Wayne wanted me to witness the truth, that he was dead.

And that's what I need you to understand, too—they are dead, both of them.

Princess Diana

The Q-Plan suggests that Princess Diana did not die in that Paris tunnel in 1997. Instead, she is supposed to be secretly married to Donald Trump, and Baron Trump is meant to be their son. As I reflect on this narrative, it occurs that Wayne deliberately orchestrated my meetings with Diana and her two sons for a specific purpose: so you would know the truth.

Diana was a double. Despite being replaced very young, she was aware of the switch. In the late '90s, Wayne took me to Angola, where we swept for landmines. Princess Diana unexpectedly appeared. She spoke passionately about how terrible landmines were and how they blew off the limbs of innocent children.

It seemed like she knew who I was, and I think she wanted to come clean. My impression of Princess Diana was that she was a genuinely kind and honest individual and hated living a life of deception. She was killed because she wanted to speak the truth about her identity.

Prince William and Prince Harry

It was around 2018 when I woke up one morning in an MK trance state. I was engrossed in my routine at home when a limousine pulled up outside. Opening the front door, I stared in disbelief as Princes William and Harry walked out, chuckling at the astonished look on my face. With a cheerful demeanor, they introduced themselves, explaining that they had just arrived from Las Vegas. Accompanying them was an agent, like Wayne, but not nearly as cool, leading me to assume they were also "under."

I whipped up some hot dogs, and we chatted in my living room. They were lots of fun, and we had a great time. For some reason, the hot dogs tasted amazingly good to all of us, which might have been part of the programming because I make hot dogs all the time, and they don't usually taste that good.

At one point in the conversation, we spoke about the queen, and Harry said, "They replaced that bitch three times!"

Then they asked about their mother. They wanted to know if their father, Prince Charles, killed her. I told them I didn't know, and they were quiet and thoughtful for a while. Then we resumed talking about other, regular things.

At some point, Wayne arrived and was listening to us. Then, as they were leaving, William attempted to put money in my coat pocket because he saw how broke I was. But Wayne took it out and handed it back to him, saying, "Yeah, it doesn't work like that."

That's all I can tell you about William and Harry. The most important takeaway, in my opinion, is that their mother is dead.

Aliens

I understand that aliens are an important part of the Q Plan. Q followers believe a group of benevolent aliens is working in league with "white hats" to provide humanity with quantum healing med-beds. I don't know anything about med-beds, and I will only describe the one experience I had with Wayne while under MK-Ultra that involved aliens.

We went into a building in New York and took an elevator deep underground. Wayne showed me to a room where there were two caskets. In each casket was a green alien, about four feet tall. I laughed, thinking they were fake and the whole thing was some prank, but when I leaned over to touch one of them, Wayne grabbed my arm and said, "Don't touch."

That's my only experience with anything relating to aliens. If I get to shake one's hand one day, I'll know they are real, but I can't offer any information beyond what I've just described.

The Border Wall Debate and a Warning from the Past

Many Americans supported the idea of Donald Trump's border wall between the U.S. and Mexico during his presidency. At the time of this writing, in 2023, the need for a wall is again being resurrected into the consciousness of concerned citizens as streams of immigrants pour into our country through the southern border. Interestingly, this mass immigration is happening before a presidential election, in which Trump is forecast to run. Undoubtedly, immigration and the erection of a wall will be one of the platforms on which he bases his campaign. But that wall will be the death of us. Wayne showed me, and so I know.

It was during the Reagan presidency, in the late 1980's, and I was in attendance at a meeting in the White House with Reagan and his cabinet. I wanted to sit at the table with everyone else, but Wayne told me to sit in the corner, watch, and listen. During the meeting, Reagan proposed a border wall, and everyone offered their opinions.

Ultimately, his military advisors told him that if the United States was invaded by China, Russia, or North Korea, that invasion would most likely happen through our Northern and coastal borders. Our only exit strategy would be through the south to Mexico. If fleeing American citizens came up against a wall, it would be a mass slaughter, the greatest holocaust the world has ever seen. Reagan understood and agreed and decided not to build the wall.

It is a matter of presidential record that this issue was visited in the past and dismissed for good reason. So now the reader must ask why this crisis—this need for a wall between us and Mexico—is being revisited and even forced. Who is Donald Trump, and what is his real agenda?

I believe Wayne showed me all these things—Donald Trump, the death of John-John, and Princess Diana—so that I could give testimony about the Q-Plan, which is quite dangerous and akin to Stalin's first five-year plan, "Operation Trust." In other instances, I believe Wayne wanted me to witness events for different reasons: to know the true nature of people in politics or entertainment and to understand aspects of important future events, many of which are currently unfolding.

In addition to witnessing the events I described, which would one day allow me to debunk the dangerous Q plan, Wayne, while under MK-Ultra, took me to observe other events related to politics and politicians. I'll share these stories here and let the reader contemplate their significance.

Nancy Pelosi and Justice Scalia

Wayne once took me to a big party where Nancy Pelosi was present. This was back when she was in her thirties. Wayne pulled her aside, and in front of me, he asked her, "Are you going to expose the truth about John here, the real John Kennedy? Or are you going to take the money and fame and power?"

Nancy cooly replied, "I'll take the money, fame, and power."

Wayne nodded like he got the answer he expected. He just wanted me to see that, to know and to understand.

Then there's Justice Scalia. Wayne took me to his cabin, a well-kept, rustic cottage with a fireplace near Marfa, Texas. An eerie silence blanketed the room where Scalia was lying in bed. He wasn't breathing, and his skin had the rubbery, white hue of a corpse. I said I thought he'd died from a heart attack, but Wayne said, "No."

Stepping forward, he pointed to one of his socks rolled down just a little bit. He pointed again, indicating for me to look closely. I squinted, and there it was—a tiny red mark, a needle puncture. Justice Scalia was killed by a hot shot to the back of his leg, and Wayne wanted me to know.

The Day I 'Shot' George Bush and Dick Cheney

Wayne must have been getting frustrated. He had big plans for me, whether it was to go into politics or run Atlantic City. I can't fathom anyone daring to defy Wayne—he generally instilled pure terror in anyone who tried.

He did that when he handed me a gun loaded with blanks and told me, "When that door swings open, I want you to shoot George Bush." So I walked around the side of the building and waited. When the door opened and Bush and Cheney walked out, I went over there and did it. I shot George Bush. Then, just for the hell of it, I shot Cheney too. Wayne wanted them to know he could take them out at any time.

Other times, Wayne used me like a decoy to find out who wanted to kill me. I remember being in a car, driving. An undercover agent sat beside me in the front seat, and some guy I didn't know was in the back. Suddenly, the guy in the back made a move to get his gun, but he never got the chance. The undercover agent whipped out his revolver and shot the guy. It blew out the back window, and human brains splattered all over the side of my face.

People knew Wayne was watching out for me, and once, when I was in my twenties, I was in Boston, and a mafia boss wanted me dead. His crew was around him, and he said, "Well, let's kill this kid."

The whole crew looked at him for a minute, then they turned their guns around and pointed them at their own boss.

They said, "We'll kill you before we kill this kid."

They went from protecting him to turning their weapons on him. I don't know what happened to that guy, but he probably just disappeared. The whole operation was meant to sniff him out and expose whose side he was on.

Amid the ongoing conflict between Russia and Ukraine, my mind drifts back to a particular incident in my early twenties. I was tagging along with Wayne in Russia, where Sylvester Stallone and Steven Seagal were filming an action movie. While under MK, Wayne took me to a museum in Ukraine. He acted furtive, as if we weren't meant to be there. But there we were, staring at these gold artifacts worth a fortune. I never entirely understood the purpose

JOHN F. KENNEDY JR.

of that visit, but it was another one of those things Wayne wanted me to witness.

Wayne was a master of MK-Ultra. It felt like he had a mysterious power that still baffles me. I'd find myself in different spots at various times without knowing how I got there. If someone ticked Wayne off, he could casually instruct them to drive their car into a fence or a fire hydrant, and they'd comply. It was like he wielded some magical control over them.

Admittedly, being Wayne's pawn wasn't my favorite thing. While I understand the purpose now, back in the day, I often resented it. As a kid, I concocted this notion of having a radio device in my head long before people knew about the full potential of brain chips and implants. I imagined they'd flick a switch, triggering me into that hypnotic state while I was asleep.

Once, during a foray into the New Jersey woods to investigate a serial killer, I spotted a transmitter attached to Wayne's car. Convinced it was the device he used to activate me, I lost it. I grabbed a branch and started beating the living daylights out of it.

I shouted at Wayne, "Go fuck yourself! What you're doing to me is totally wrong." I ranted on, beating that thing to a pulp.

MK-Ultra quietly infiltrates the lives of everyday citizens more than they imagine. Many people know about the subliminal messaging strategically embedded in movies, TV shows, and advertisements. Many are familiar with the viral video exposing the mockingbird media. Newscasters nationwide echoed the same words from identical scripts, a synchronized chorus that culminated in a crescendo of them chanting in unison, *"...which is very dangerous for our democracy."*

Yet, how many are aware that twenty-two military veterans take their own lives every day? That's 8,030 well-trained, able-bodied soldiers lost each year—individuals who could stand ready to defend our country in the event of an invasion.

During basic training, I was forced to peer into binoculars placed on top of a massive spinning cylinder, racing through images at 1,000 miles an hour. All I saw was blood, guts, and gore, images that haunted me and drove me toward suicidal thoughts. The only reason I didn't do it is because I remembered the words of Victor, the same guy who was later involved in an encounter with Max Jr. where they tried to kill me outside a shopping mall.

Victor once said, "If you ever think of killing yourself, don't. We need you around."

That was the interesting thing about Victor. He was some double agent. Maybe he's why I didn't get killed that day when Max Jr. set me up.

But I can't help but think that many of our military personnel ending their lives underwent similar MK-Ultra suicide programming. This should clearly indicate that our government has been overthrown and replaced by a shadowy, treacherous regime. If one of their goals is to dismantle our military through suicide programming and other covert methods, it is cause for grave concern.

Imagine a scenario where a criminal spy in the White House could easily direct our military in the wrong direction in the event of an invasion. The implications are chilling.

BOOK TWO

KILLERS, KIDNAPPINGS, AND HOLLYWOOD

BROKEN DREAMS

"Always remember who you are," my mother, Jackie, once said. "Your father was a United States president."

The Secret Service introduced my mother's body doubles early on. The main one, shown in photographs with Aristotle and in later pictures taken in New York, was present from the start and even appears in some early pictures taken at the White House. They were rotated so frequently that I couldn't tell the difference sometimes. But I remember the most prominent double once saying, "I'm not quitting smoking for anybody." And so you can often distinguish between her and my mother as the double wears oversized sunglasses and smokes.

My real mother loved art and painting. When I was little, Jackie sent me to study with various artists. I went to Israel to study with

Chagall for a few weeks and to Chicago to study with Picasso. He was working on metal crafts then, and my job was to polish the metal for him. I was with a bunch of kids, and I remember us all sitting around a picnic table with paper and pencils, learning how to sketch the flower or whatever still life was in front of us.

One famous artist threw a big fit about having to teach me. He didn't want to do it. He was yelling and arguing, and I tried to tune it out by focusing on a picture on his wall. It was of me on my mother's lap. In the picture, I am two or three years old, and I'm playing with her pearls. She is laughing, with her head flung back. When John-John and Carolyn sold my mother's belongings at Sotheby's Auction House, that one picture sold for $150,000, and it wasn't even his! It breaks my heart to think of how that picture went to a stranger.

Not long after my father's death, my mother took me and my sister, Caroline, to The United Kingdom. I remember several things about that trip. I remember my mother arguing with the queen in an ornate parlor at Buckingham Palace. The argument had something to do with my father, and my mother said, "You bitch!" The Queen wrinkled her nose and said haughtily, "Oh, you're a bitch."

Wayne accompanied us on that trip. It was our first covert military operation together. He took me to Ireland, where he met some high-ups in the Irish Republican Army.

Upon arrival, our car parked in front of a small stone house, where a guide greeted us. Venturing into the depths of interconnected basements, we eventually found ourselves outdoors, navigating planks over muddy ground to yet another home with a basement. It was in this dim, musty space that we had our meeting with the IRA.

Seated at a worn table, the Irish resistance fighters told me, a child, how they couldn't find work or provide for their families. I understood that it was poverty and hunger that fueled their resentment towards England. When we returned to England, I spoke to the queen about it.

I said, "Look, these people are just hungry. You have to help them. Do what you can do because they are willing to fight for their families so that they can eat."

The queen thanked me and gifted me a ring. It was a pretty ugly ring, with a green stone veined with mossy tendrils. I felt disappointed that it wasn't nicer, but I was still happy to get it. Unfortunately, someone took it away, and I never saw it again.

Our official tour included visiting an orphanage in Scotland, where President Eisenhower was also in attendance. Secret Service agents told Caroline and me to stand against a brick wall to one side of a wooden doorway. Across from us, I could see a young girl with light brown hair cut in a pageboy crying at a picnic table. I pointed her out to my mother, who encouraged me to go over and comfort her. I could hardly understand what she was saying through her tears, but her nurse informed me that she came from an aristocratic family, and they had been murdered in front of her. Now, no one knew what to do with her.

I approached my mother and said, "We have to help this girl."

She agreed and arranged for the girl to be adopted by an American family in Phoenix, Arizona, who changed her name to Brenda.

Brenda and I stayed in touch over the years. We found one another because we both lived in the same witness protection area, and we called ourselves "The Children of Murdered Parents Club." I don't know what happened to her with her new family, but she can't remember her first years with them and was left only with a lingering sense that her mother wasn't her real mother and that things weren't quite right. Sadly, she turned to drugs and was addicted to heroin for much of her adult life. She died in 2021.

1968 was the year Bobby was killed, and my mother married Aristotle Onassis. I was with Jackie and a government agent at a motel when Bobby was shot. I believe this was the fake Jackie because the two of them were talking about the other John being somewhere and that something was going to happen, but I didn't understand it then. It just felt like they were planning something.

After it happened, however, I remember my real mother crying her eyes out for hours. "I'm going to too many funerals," she sobbed.

That's all I remember about Bobby's murder. I don't remember the funeral, just my mother's tears.

The Kennedy family was being systematically destroyed through murder, identity theft, and trauma. After Bobby died, I witnessed my mother being raped on an airplane on our way to New York. We were traveling with Jackie and her double. In the middle of the flight, a big, menacing man on the plane started assaulting her, and I was in tears, completely freaking out. The other men on the plane threatened that if I didn't quiet down, they'd kill her.

When the plane landed, I was trembling. Everything seemed like fragmented snapshots, a disjointed reality. Someone handed me a dog on a leash and said, "You're getting off the plane with this dog to meet your new sister."

I looked at him blankly and said, "I don't have a new sister."

The fake Jackie exited the plane with me, wearing glasses and a big smile for the cameras. A girl approached me, dressed like my other sister.

I said, "You're not real. You're fake."

With eerie calmness, she said, "I know I'm not, but you better go along with it."

It unnerved me how composed, and collectedly she stepped into my sister's role. She acted like Hollywood had schooled her to act like my sister.

By this point, I was crying uncontrollably. A policeman approached me and said, "Hey John, I knew your father. He was a good president. I want to thank you. Is there anything I can do to help you?"

I said, "Yeah, you can help me. They're going to kill my mother. I've got a new sister. There's plenty you can do to help me out."

When he heard that, he approached the pilot and said, "The kid's not going with the program."

That didn't go over very well. They took me back on the airplane, and the same agent who raped my mother started beating and kicking me. I fell to the ground, and he kept kicking and stomping me. I don't know if someone stopped him or what happened—because I was sure he would kill me—but I blacked out.

After the rape and Bobby's murder, my mother was suffering from extreme mental turmoil and seeking solace and answers through different spiritual paths. It was during this phase that she decided to take me to India. There, I remember riding camels with a group of Indian men who were believers in an unusual spiritual practice. According to them, if an elephant gave birth to a child, they were considered to be born again as the child of the Elephant God. So that's what happened.

They found an elephant that had recently given birth, and two men pushed me up the elephant's vagina into her womb. Instantly, I couldn't breathe. I was suffocating and panicking, trying to fight my way out of there. Finally, the elephant pushed me out, and I fell about four feet to the ground, covered in goo.

Everyone ran over to make sure I was alright, but I felt like hell for three or four minutes. I just sat there, trying to breathe, staring at them in disbelief, shocked that they'd actually done that. But sometimes, as a joke, when someone asks, who's your mother? I shrug and respond, "The Elephant God."

At different times with the Quigleys, Federal agents would show up, and bring me to Aristotle's private island. No one ever gave me any advance notice. I remember one time Dorothy Quigley took me shopping for boating shoes, and the next thing I knew, I was being flown to Greece for a trip on Aristotle's yacht, *The Christina*.

An early memory of that time is walking on board Aristotle's yacht at night. The sky was clear, and the stars shone brightly like a blanket of darkness adorned with twinkling jewels. My mother looked up and pointed at one exceptionally bright star and said, "Remember that star as your father, looking over us." I always remember that.

I also remember my new siblings, Christina and Alexander. I loved them and admired Alexander so much! I remember one of his birthdays at the airport, where a convoy of black limousines, like a presidential motorcade, rolled by where we stood on the runway. Suddenly, a Jaguar pulled up, and Aristotle stepped out and dropped the keys into Alexander's hand with a big smile, saying, "Happy birthday, Son."

When I was on the island, I'd go fishing and try to catch dinner. There was a maintenance man who kept things running, and he became my friend, helping me clean the fish I caught. I also remember finding ancient pottery shards and bringing them to my mother on the beach. I'd say, "Hey, Mom, check this out!"

Nighttime on the island meant parties with Hollywood stars, artists, and influential people. The island was also the only place I saw my sister after my father's death, but we didn't have much to do with one another. I would be off swimming, and she was off doing her own thing. I loved her, but she was kind of bitchy to me. Once, she showed up on crutches. I think she broke her leg skiing or something like that.

I said, "Oh, what happened?"

But she snapped back. "Oh, shut up."

On some of those trips, they had a Caroline look-alike. Jackie and Aristotle insisted it was my sister, and honestly, I got so fed up and confused that I stopped caring. I think the last time I saw my actual sister, she was between ten and twelve years old. After that, she vanished from my life, and I have no idea what happened to her.

My mother married Aristotle on the Island of Skorpios in 1968 when I was eight. I remember a few things about that wedding. Jackie and Aristotle drank out of special cups, like Russian wedding eggs, and Aristotle said, "I don't believe these are real gold. I think that jeweler ripped me off." Then he went off in search of someone to speak to the jeweler.

In addition to being on the island, Aristotle took me to Saudi Arabia once. We sat in a circle, smoking a hookah, and they told me I was their stepson because I was Aristotle's new son. I couldn't understand most of what they were saying—half the time, it was in Greek or Arabic—but after that, they conducted a couple of ceremonies and assured me that if anything ever happened, I could return. They would protect me because I was one of them now.

While I can't recall their names and wouldn't know whom to contact if I was in trouble, it was still very cool.

Another thrilling thing we did was go on archeological digs. Once, we went with Aristotle, Wayne, my mother, and a group of other people to the site of the tomb of Alexander the Great's father, Philip II of Macedon, located in the mountains of Northern Greece. There were amazing artifacts, but the people I was with looted the place. Among the items were tons of platinum and gold pieces and devices of ancient technology that could be compared to modern computers in terms of function. These artifacts were like circular disks with numerical inscriptions that stored information. Some artifacts used precious gems and metals to create holograms and moving pictures. All those artifacts went to the family. What the public got to see was what they considered the rubbish remains.

I believe Illuminati families gain access to advanced technology long before it reaches the public. Experiences like the one I had on this dig lead me to believe that a substantial portion of this technology has ancient origins, potentially linked to a prior, more advanced civilization. The know-how for constructing this technology needs to be conveyed discreetly for some reason.

As a boy, I recall sitting on the floor of Bill Gates' garage as he was building his first computer. I held one of two small, yellow Walkie-Talkies Wayne and I purchased at Sears. Whenever Bill got stuck, he would ask me to consult Wayne. I would relay Bill's question over the Walkie-Talkie and then convey Wayne's responses.

The times I spent on Aristotle's Island are some of my best memories. I wish I could go back there and swim in the lagoon. But those days came to a tragic end. It was on one of my trips to Greece that my step-brother, Alexander Onassis, was murdered.

I was thirteen. Jackie, Aristotle, Alexander, and I were walking through the airport in Skorpios. Alexander said he was going to take his plane on a short trip, and I said, "I want to go! Can I come?"

"Not today, kid," Alexander replied.

But I was insistent. "Please, Please let me come!"

Finally, he relented and told me to meet him on the runway.

When I got down there, however, the plane was already moving.

I panicked, thinking he was leaving without me, and ran after the aircraft's tail, where I knew a hatch door was located for stocking the plane with food and liquor. I reached it in time and climbed in.

I crawled into the cockpit and then froze at the scene before me. Alexander sat there, sweat rolling down his face. Barely breathing, his eyes were wide with fear. To his side, a mechanic I recognized held a rusty revolver pressed to my brother's temple. Unable to move or speak, my mind raced, turning over plans to rescue Alexander.

"Fly," commanded the mechanic.

The plane lifted about thirty feet, and the movement unglued my tongue.

Without thinking, I blurted out, "That thing won't fire!"

Both of them gasped. In an attempt to face me, Alexander began to turn, but before his gaze could meet mine, the mechanic pulled the trigger, sending a bullet straight into Alexander's temple.

Alexander's head snapped to the side, then slumped forward. The plane nosedived toward the ground, and I screamed, clawing at the upholstery, tearing it apart with my fingernails. The aircraft collided with the runway, a thunderous crash echoing like an exploding furnace. My body bounced and twisted, a sharp, searing pain shooting through my arm. In the moment that followed the crash, all I could hear was my own ragged breathing.

Propelled by frantic urgency, I crawled forward. The mechanic lay unconscious, and there, Alexander, a sizable bullet hole in his head, lay lifeless. I pulled him onto my lap, tears streaming down my face as the distant wail of sirens drew near.

The following chaotic scene was filled with shouts and tearing sounds as rescue personnel used tools to pry open the fuselage. It took them fifteen minutes to cut through the wreckage. The whole time, they kept trying to reassure me, saying, "Hang on, hold on, we're coming." All I could do was cry, watch them work, and gaze at Alexander through a blurry cataract of tears.

The next thing I remember is waking up in the hospital. Aristotle barged into my room, gripped my arm, and hurled me against the wall. His voice boomed and crackled like a loudspeaker with frayed wires.

Vehemently, he warned me, "You can never, ever tell anyone that your brother was shot. Not ever. People will think the family is weak, and we will not be safe."

The next day, he went to a judge and ordered him to sign the death warrant, declaring Alexander's death an accident. They hanged the mechanic, but they kept Alexander's dead body in a hospital room for a day so they could pretend he died from his injuries. Christina came and sat beside his bed, mourning his death.

An autopsy followed, and I vividly recall the doctor mentioning they found the bullet, describing how it "spun around in his brain." That haunting image of a bullet spinning in Alexander's head became a lasting picture in my mind.

Over the next few days, mercenaries armed with machine guns ran all over the island. Aristotle was highly paranoid, and he carried binoculars everywhere, scanning the horizon for potential threats. Crouched at the bottom of a staircase, I huddled with my mother and her sister, Aunt Lee Radzwill, who was visiting. Lee's voice was filled with terror.

"I want to go home!" She cried. "We're all going to die on this island."

After Alexander died, I remember sitting with Christina at a picnic table. My arm was in a cast, and I was trying to get her to talk to me. She was crying and in shock and wouldn't move or speak.

Then she turned on me and said, "How come you have no remorse for my brother? Did you kill my brother?"

I was thirteen and didn't know how to respond. I remembered Aristotle's warning.

All I could manage to say was, "You have to talk to your father. Ask him, please!"

After that, we boarded the yacht and sailed for weeks. I had to stay in my cabin and couldn't put my head above deck in case someone saw me. When we finally docked, my legs wobbled so badly from being at sea I could barely make it down the long path back to our home in Skorpios.

When we got back to the island, I was confronted by three of Caroline's doubles. One of them said, "We're going to kill you. You're not the real John Kennedy Jr."

Stunned, I stammered, "What?"

I was so confused. I don't know what happened to my real sister, but I learned from Alexander's death that the families don't want to admit when one of their own is killed. They think it makes them look weak. But I think that's what happened to Caroline. The beautiful, vivacious sister that I knew in early childhood died a long, long time ago. I don't know when or how, but I would guess it was before my mother married Aristotle because it was both Jackie and Caroline's doubles at their wedding. I'm not sure if Jackie not being at her wedding and Caroline being missing or dead are connected, but it was around that time that my mother started to lose her mind.

On one visit to New York, the Secret Service orchestrated a photo op with John-John and me riding bikes in Central Park. A photographer snapped pictures of us separately and together while the anxious Secret Service agents scurried around nervously. The looks on their faces said, "I can't believe we're doing this."

All the while, my mother, Jackie, sat on the hood of a car, reading a book, and I kept wondering why she wouldn't come and spend time with me. But by then, they had scrambled her brains pretty badly with LSD, bullying, and trauma. She didn't speak to me at all that day.

Another vivid memory is when I found her painting a giraffe against a blue background for Caroline's room. She was spaced out, and I couldn't communicate with her. I kept saying, "Mom, what's wrong with you? What's wrong with you?"

She looked at me, eyes wide with surprise, and said, "Who are you?"

My stomach dropped, and I could only stare at her, speechless and afraid. Later, I came to know that feeling of not knowing who I was when trauma and torture left me so scatterbrained I didn't know my own name. On one such occasion, she gave me a compass, saying, "It's so you'll never lose your way."

Christina was also driven insane through bullying, trauma, and God knows what else. I have a picture of her with one of the Kennedys, and in it, he's gripping her arm while pointing a warning finger at her, like he's telling her what to do. She appears visibly distraught and is crying. I remember that scene. I approached her and asked, "What happened? Please tell me what happened." But she kept insisting she couldn't say.

Finally, she broke down and said, "They made me kill my own father."

However, I suspect it was a body double, as the real Aristotle met his end later. He was brutally murdered with a camping ax in the sideyard of our Bullhead, Arizona home.

Years later, a similar scenario unfolded in 1975 when they staged an elaborate scene to convince me that the murdered Martha Moxley was my sister. Under MK-Ultra, they can make you believe you murdered Minnie Mouse.

Christina, a sweet soul but somewhat naive, married a Russian she believed loved her. Once, at a lavish party on the yacht, I overheard her husband discussing her murder with friends. Frantically, I approached Christina.

I said, "Christina, I have to talk to you. It's very important."

She said, "Don't bother me, kid."

I said, "No, no, you really need to hear me. Okay, I heard your husband talking about killing you. I love you. I don't want to see you dead. You have to know."

She looked at me, and I could tell she believed me. Then she stalked over to where her husband sat and confronted him in front of everyone.

She said, "What's this I hear? You're trying to have me murdered?"

Years later, I heard about Christina's death from an overdose and that her father had left her 70 million dollars. That's when I realized she must have been murdered and replaced. Aristotle had billions. He would not have left Christina a mere 70 million. After Christina's death, the island of Skorpios went to the Russians.

I never returned to Aristotle's Island after Alexander's death. Instead, I was sent back to the Quigley family while Jackie and Aristotle established a stronghold in Bullhead City, Arizona. They bought up the town and put their people in all the houses in the area with the help of their trusted confidante, Don Laughlin, a casino owner in Las Vegas. Laughlin would later betray Jackie and Aristotle, however, to further line his pockets and expand his empire.

From the age of nine, the Secret Service constantly switched out me and my body double. Except for some rare occasions at school, they ensured we were never seen in the same spot. When he was in New York, I was likely on the island, and vice versa—creating a carefully crafted illusion. There were a few times when we were together, however.

Once, when I was on a speedboat with the fake Caroline and John-John on a lake somewhere in the Northeast, Caroline turned to me and said, "Listen, we don't want to hang around with you anymore. They want us to murder you, and I don't want to."

John-John remained silent, but I knew that when someone tells you you're going to die, they want you dead. The thing is, these doubles are put in when they're too young to know anything themselves. John-John did turn out to be an evil man, but Caroline's double had enough conscience to warn me.

HOLLYWOOD

Wayne was an enigmatic guardian who watched over my life, keeping me safe and exposing me to the world of Hollywood, the music business, the casino business, the military, and the government. Viewing me as one of the only living heirs to the Kennedy family, he wanted me to understand the ins and outs of all the lines in the family business.

One of my early experiences with Hollywood occurred when I was around ten or eleven. Wayne picked me up from the Quigley's and drove me to the set of the police drama, *Adam-12*. In that episode, I played the role of a boy whose head got stuck between the bars of a fence. The officers had to slather my head with grease to get me out. My spoken part was, "My mom's sure gonna be mad at me when I get home." The whole thing was over in about fifteen minutes, then I wiped the goop from my head, and Wayne took me back home.

After that, I had short appearances in shows like *Mayber-ry-RFD*, *Daniel Boone*, and *The Courtship of Eddie's Father*.

Another cool memory from the entertainment world was being taken to Lady Gaga's house when she was just a little kid. She was playing on a toy xylophone, hitting the colored keys with a little mallet.

I said, "Wow, you're pretty good at that."

I didn't realize it, but someone taped the interaction, and if you listen to the Eagles' CD *Hotel California*, a track at the end features a kid playing the xylophone and a boy saying, "You're pretty good at that." That's me and Lady Gaga.

Wayne also brought me to the studio where AC/DC recorded the *Ballbreaker* album. On the album, there's a song called "Hail Caesar." While I was there, they had me practicing that song re-peatedly for hours until my throat got sore. Then, when the final version was produced, they dubbed in my voice. I don't know why they did that, but I always listen to it. Once, I was driving with Brenda, and it came on the radio. I started singing, and she looked at me wide-eyed.

"Hey, it *is* you!" She said with surprise.

I chuckled and said, "Yeah, that's me. I wasn't lying."

Wayne also had me working on Hollywood sets, and I remember that big movie stars like Clint Eastwood, John Wayne, and Charles Bronson had crews of guys that followed them around. They were in serious competition with each other, and I remember once

Charles Bronson told me to go to the restaurant across the street and get him a beer but insisted I had to bring it back with the top on.

I went to get it, but the woman behind the counter removed the cap. I tried to tell her to give me another one, but she refused, so I brought it over to Bronson, and he was pissed.

He said, "I'm not drinking this. You go tell her to give you one with the top on."

He was afraid of getting poisoned, and I did as he said.

Charles Bronson had his crew, and Clint Eastwood had his crew—each star had his little entourage. John Wayne could gather twenty or thirty men together and beat somebody up. It was that cutthroat. They all wanted money and parts in movies.

Once, I was on a movie set with John Wayne in California, and there was a gold mine next to us.

I said, "Hey, John, can I look for gold in that gold mine?"

He replied, "You know what kid? You can make more money in the movies than you'll ever make digging in that hole over there."

Another incident involved a guy on the set picking on me to the point of pushing me to the ground. Seeing what was happening, John Wayne got his crew together, and the next thing I knew, the whole entourage was over there in a big circle kicking the crap out of that guy.

Many houses in Yosemite Lakes, where the Quigleys lived, were owned by Hollywood people. Among them were Clint Eastwood and Richard Kiel, famous as Jaws in James Bond movies. I did some work for Kiel during one of his film projects.

One day, I visited a classmate's lavish brick house, where he had a room transformed into an Elvis Presley shrine. Hundreds of Elvis records adorned the walls and dangled from strings attached to the ceiling—a miniature Elvis museum.

He said, "My dad was Elvis Presley. We're waiting on a lot of money, and then we're getting out of here."

He told me how his mom and Elvis hooked up on a movie set, and the estate owed him a lot of money for being Elvis's son.

I never saw that kid or his family again after that. The next thing I knew, Richard Kiel moved into his house. The family just disappeared.

I got to meet Elvis myself a couple of times, once in Hawaii and once at Graceland. During our visit to Graceland, Elvis planned a ride on trikes—big, three-wheel motorcycles. Elvis had paid some guy 5,000 dollars to design a unique heating suit, with pipes channeling engine heat into the hood of his jacket. It was a really crazy contraption, and I couldn't help laughing when I sat down behind him; he just looked so funny!

Unfortunately, a woman came running out of the house before we could get going and said I couldn't go with him. I wasn't allowed to leave the property and had to go back inside. A photographer snapped a picture of me—with my head turned to hide my identity—but I remember that day well.

Elvis and me. (R.I.P. Sonny 81~ Much respect, John Kennedy Jr.)

The mob made good on their promise to Denzel. He became a big Hollywood star, but Wayne wanted to show me how he turned out, so he dropped me off at the set where they were rehearsing, *Training Day.* The moment I arrived, a group of guys grabbed me, punched me, drugged me, tossed me into a bathtub, and put a gun in my mouth.

I was sure they were going to blow my head off. I was under MK-Ultra and was thinking, "What the hell?" Then they started practicing their lines from the movie, and when I saw it in the theater, I was shocked. They had enacted a scene from the film, using me as their victim. I think Wayne dropped me off to show me what a fuck-up Denzel turned out to be and that I shouldn't trust him.

KIDNAPPED

I was kidnapped a few times in those days. To the feds, I was a walking ATM: *Hey, let's kidnap Jackie Kennedy's kid and score a few million dollars*, is how they thought. It was a game to them. The very government agents that were assigned to protect me would turn into kidnappers. Then, they'd call my mother and say, "Jackie, John's kidnapped. We need so much money to secure his release."

The first time it happened was when I was living with the Quigleys in Clovis. A government agent came to the house, and I was happy to see him, thinking we would finally get to the bottom of this Kennedy stuff. Instead, he took me to a house in a subdivision, probably in Fresno, California.

We got out of the car, and he said, "Come on with me," so we walked to the backyard. As soon as we got out back, a guy came running up to me and started punching me—*boom, boom, boom*—right in the face. He beat me up badly. Then, both of them told me to take off my bloody shirt, put on a green soccer shirt, and get in a dog cage. They took a photograph of me and sent it to Aristotle for ransom money.

The whole time I was in there, I kept repeating to myself, "Out of the darkness, into the light."

At some point, they made me take a handful of pills, and I don't remember anything after that, just waking up at the Quigleys.

On another occasion, I was locked in a bathroom for days. I thought I was going to die. I don't think they even fed me. Lying on the floor, I scratched into the baseboard: "I'm John Kennedy Jr., and I was here." I thought if they killed me, at least somebody would know I was there. I don't remember how old I was then.

But the most horrific kidnapping incident happened when I studied with an artist in Spain. He was painting me, and a guy came in and took me. He identified himself as an agent who was supposed to pick me up and take me back to Jackie.

He ushered me into his car and drove to a little house in the countryside. Inside, he placed a plate with rat poison-laced rice and beans in front of me and told me he'd shoot me if I didn't eat it. A Spanish girl watched us warily as I ate the poisoned food while his gun was pointed at my head. I could tell she wanted to help but didn't dare, and I obediently spooned the bitter mixture into my mouth and forced myself to swallow.

After I ate it, he left, and I got very ill. I was lying on the floor of this dirty house, clutching my stomach in pain and crying. The

Spanish woman brought over a trash can and made me throw up in it. It helped a little, but I was still lying on the floor when some Spanish officials—police or government agents—came in, grabbed me, and put me in a pickup truck.

We were traveling on a dirt road when some headlights came at us. Both vehicles stopped. The guy from the other car got out and started coming towards us. That's when the agent I was with pulled out a gun, flipped the door open and shot the guy in the head.

Then he got back in the car and drove us to the cartel. There was a big corral there, and I recognized the woman who had helped me throw up into the trash can. One of the cartel members grabbed her by the arm and said, "We're going to feed her to the lions." They thought she was part of the plot to kidnap me.

I said, "No man, you can't feed her to the lions. She tried to save my life. She helped me."

He shrugged. "My lions 'gotta eat. They're hungry."

After some back and forth, they decided not to worry about it until the next day. I was so sick I passed out on a cot until morning, when the government agent woke me up and told me to stand by the corral fence.

Spanish villagers lined the fence, watching as a growling, restless lion paced back and forth. Soon, an elderly man was tossed into the enclosure. With a barbaric grip, the lion clamped onto his stomach, shaking him violently like a dog with a chew toy. I can't remember what happened after that.

The other incident that stands out in my memory was a kidnapping attempt in Mexico orchestrated by the Quigleys. Dorothy, Max Quigley, and Dorothy's brother, Richard Crisp, decided we would all drive down to Mexico because Richard wanted to see a show where a woman has sex with a donkey.

Upon our arrival in Mexico, we got out of a taxi in the middle of a bustling marketplace with street vendors and children peddling candy and gum. We were all standing in the street, and I started to feel peculiar like they all knew something I didn't and were waiting for something to happen. Eager to get away from them, I spotted a tent selling firecrackers and asked if I could explore. They said, "Sure, go ahead."

As I wandered within the store, a Mexican man suddenly pulled out a knife and started walking toward me. I stood frozen, but the store owner swiftly came up behind him, seizing the guy's hand that was holding the knife and grabbing his throat with his other hand. I understood what he was saying, that he was going to kill the guy with his own knife, and I ran out of the store and searched for the Quigleys.

When I told them what happened, they just looked at each other, shrugged, and muttered in subdued tones, "I can't believe he got out of that one."

BOOK THREE

MURDER AND BLACK OPS

1975: THE DARKEST CHAPTER

After Alexander's death, I returned to the Quigleys, while Jackie and Aristotle carved out a domain in Bullhead City, Arizona, a small desert town nestled along the Colorado River. They strategically acquired the town, placing their people in every available house.

Then, in 1975, when I was fifteen years old, I was picked up from the Quigleys and brought there. My heart got lighter with every mile we traveled. Finally, I was getting away! My joy even grew when the landscape transformed from lush greenery and palm tree-lined roads to arid brown soil punctuated by clusters of thorny shrubs, sucking the last remnants of moisture from the dusty earth.

In the late afternoon, the car pulled up in front of a modest vanilla ranch-style home atop a hill boasting a gently sloping lawn adorned with a few palm trees. The inside was filled with lavish furnishings for a larger, grander home. Aristotle boasted about how he had installed air conditioning, and we talked about changing our names and starting again.

Jackie envisioned a life where I could work in a garage, fixing cars. She was excited to start a new life with her family and forget about all the criminal corruption. But out of caution, they arranged for a camper trailer near the service station, my potential refuge in case I needed to hide out.

At first, it seemed like it would work out. Jackie and Aristotle liked the desert. They were nudists and enjoyed taking off their clothes and walking around in the hot, dry air. There was a movie theater in the town where many Hollywood stars came to practice and audition, even though it didn't have power. Actors, producers, and directors gathered in the building at night and put on productions, using candles and reflectors to illuminate the stage. I remember many people being there who, to this day, are big Hollywood stars.

One day, I was sitting by the ravine in the middle of the desert, using a kit I had to pan for gold. It was dead quiet except for the sound of burbling water, buzzing insects, and the occasional whisk of a lizard darting through the grass. Suddenly, a handful of kids came walking towards me. They ranged in age from about eight to eighteen. The eldest was a boy holding a video recorder. He was a smart ass.

He said, "We're from Hollywood. We're making a movie, and you're not invited."

I shrugged and returned to my panning. It seemed weird, but I was used to weirdness. It wasn't until I got home that I saw what kind of movie they had been making.

My stepfather, Aristotle Onassis, lay dead in the sideyard, covered by a bloody sheet, having been bludgeoned repeatedly with a camping ax that now lay next to his body. The kids were gone, but about four agents were standing there, discussing what they would do and how they would send him back to Greece. I wanted to go over to Aristotle, but they held me back. One of them picked up the ax.

I started crying uncontrollably. I couldn't believe Aristotle, a powerful, forceful man who seemed invincible, lay dead and lifeless under that sheet. All my hopes and dreams for the future bled out of me like the seeping red stain on the sheet and grass. I waited for someone to come over and say something to me, but they ignored me, and their voices blended like the buzz of cicadas just before dark.

It was typical mob tactics, I realized with despair. Each kid probably had to take a turn hitting Aristotle with the axe while that older boy videotaped it. That way, the mafia would have a murder rap on all those kids who would later become Hollywood movie stars and money-makers for the syndicate.

My mother came home later, and what happened next was blocked from my memory. Sometimes, screams are soundless, like the echoing silence after a sonic boom.

Amidst the grief and pandemonium that followed, Jackie was scared something would happen to me, so she told me to hide in a local restaurant. In a secluded room, I overheard the restaurant owner speaking in a frightened voice on the phone.

"I don't want him here. He comes here all the time. They'll know he's here." The next day, the restaurant burned to the ground, and I relocated to my trailer next to the service station. Then Jackie sent me to Greenwich, Connecticut, to stay with some Kennedys.

I was at a house I'd been to before, where the Kennedy kids were always mean to me. One Kennedy boy—a really nasty kid—would routinely pummel me, so I hated going there. That day, about six of us kids were playing Monopoly in the house. An elderly bald man in his sixties came in with a golf club and beckoned us to follow him outside.

"Come on, kids," he said.

They all got up to follow him as if the whole thing had been prearranged, but then he turned around and pointed at me.

"Not you, kid. You stay in the house."

Feeling singled out and excluded, I waited for them to leave before settling on the sofa, sensing that something was off. Suddenly, a truck pulled up to the house. I went outside to see who it was, and a federal agent instructed me to get inside. Behind the wheel sat another agent, and inside the truck were my mother and a man with a gun pointed at her head. Paralyzed with terror, my heart thudded. I looked at her, unable to utter a word. Fear gleamed in her eyes as they darted nervously between me and the road ahead.

We drove to a yard where a girl's dead body lay beneath a pine tree, her long, blonde hair obscuring her face. A broken, bloody golf club lay beside her in the grass. A federal agent held me by one arm, pointed at the body, and said, "That's your sister."

I felt like someone threw me into a swirling tunnel of insanity. Everything was moving around me, but I was as still as a footprint in the grass as anger, grief, and horror coursed silently through me. At the same time, I had a niggling sensation of something like deja vù. I thought, "I've seen this before, done this before."

MK-Ultra sometimes involves repetition. This scene was replayed twice. The first time, I was in an MK trance state, hearing discussions about placing a body, as if the agents there were setting up a crime scene and planting ideas in my head. They may have shown me my actual sister's dead body or a convincing look-alike.

The thought was quickly jettisoned from my mind when the federal agent said, "Now, here's what you're going to do, kid. You're going to pick up that golf club and stab your sister with it, or else we'll kill your mother. I'll be waiting in the truck."

He walked away, and I stood there, my insides heaving. I knew I couldn't do it. I thought, "I'll just tell them I did it."

I returned to the truck, and when I got in, I went completely wild. I leaped over my mother and scratched the agent's face, screaming and crying hysterically. They tried to calm me down, but I went completely nuts.

When the Martha Moxley murder story broke in the news, I was convinced that it was my sister and that Martha Moxley was her undercover name in the witness protection program. For years, I never questioned the idea. Martha Moxley was my dead sister.

I went crazy that day, and that notion stayed with me for many years. They wanted me to believe it, and it isn't easy to understand why. Perhaps they wanted me never to wonder or investigate what happened to my real sister.

In the panic and hysteria that followed Aristotle's murder and the Martha Moxley incident, my mother was sure I was next on the hit list and asked Wayne if he could get me out of the country to keep me safe. I don't know what they were thinking—as I said, these people operate in a world of crazy—but it was decided that Wayne would take me to Vietnam.

We drove to an airfield where uniformed personnel were heaving sacks of mail into the belly of an army cargo plane. Wayne told me to climb on top of the canvas sacks, and then he settled into the cockpit. We flew for hours. Finally, we landed on a dirt runway nestled in the dense jungle.

Wayne indicated a group of soldiers and said, "Go with these guys. They're going to teach you everything." He pointed a warning finger at me and added, "And whatever happens, don't tell anyone who you are."

From that point, the soldiers taught me all the skills to help me stay alive in the jungle, like using a knife to cut off branches. I remember eating army food, which was terrible, like cardboard. Eventually, we met up with their unit and went out on patrol.

They said, "Don't ever talk. Don't ever ask a question. Just shut your mouth."

"...or we'll kill you." Another guy added.

Tommy was a wiry kid with hard eyes. He liked to kill people with his long machete. When it got covered in blood, he licked it off and said, "I like to taste my enemies."

One day, we were all eating lunch beside a pile of dead bodies. The soldiers were going through their packs, and one of them pulled out a bundle of leather straps. This guy's father was a congressman, and he said his dad told him to always have a bunch of these straps on hand because they come in handy.

Tommy looked at him and nodded. Then he handed me his pocket knife and said, "Hey kid, go and cut the ears off those bodies over there."

I knew I had to do it. I had to do everything they told me. I put my food on the ground in slow motion, stood up, and walked over with the pocket knife. "Don't think," I told myself, and I started cutting off the ears and placing them in a neat pile.

The funny thing about cutting off other people's ears is that you can't hear anything out of your own—just a loud, roaring sound, like wind blowing on fire. I jumped when I felt something thin and snake-like fall around my neck. When I jerked my head around, Tommy was standing there, grinning.

He said, "We'll make you an ear necklace."

He took the ears I'd already cut off, slid the leather strap through them, and tied it off before hanging it around my neck.

As he turned to walk away, he said over his shoulder, "Keep cutting."

After I'd cut off a few more, the commander came by and asked what we were doing.

"You can't do that!" He said. "You have to put those ears back." He shook his head slowly as if pondering the situation. After a sigh, he unbuttoned his breast pocket and pulled out a small plastic case. Snapping it open, he asked, "You know how to sew, kid?"

I shook my head and shivered despite the heat and humidity. The commander inclined his head for me to watch him as he took out a needle and thread from the case and sewed an ear back on. The only thing was—and I guess this was meant to be the funny part—he sewed it on backward.

I took a deep breath and bent over the dead, earless bodies. Then I started sewing those ears back on the heads, backward, my ear-neckless bouncing against my chest as I worked. There was a big commotion while I was doing that, and everyone started getting their gear together quickly.

We headed off through the jungle, and as we passed some bushes, one of the soldiers gave me a shove and said, "Get under there and don't make a sound. Don't come out until we come for you."

I scrambled under the bush, terrified as shots, shells, and shouts sounded in the distance. Day grew into night, and no one came for me. Eventually, the sounds of fighting died down, but I was too terrified to move. I stayed under there most of the next day. By this time, I had pissed and shit myself, and my legs were numb.

Finally, an eerie silence fell over the area, punctuated by an occasional, far-off voice echo, but I couldn't tell if it was American or Vietnamese. Eventually, I heard a helicopter, and the thought twanged into my head like a released arrow: "It's now or never."

Grunting with the pain of trying to move my deadened legs, I rolled out from under the bush and ran towards the helicopter. My brain was so scattered that I didn't know who I was or what I was doing. After seeing all the dead bodies, Tommy licking the knife, and then putting the ears on a rope, all I could do was run to the chopper. I didn't know if it was ours or theirs, but I knew I couldn't stay where I was. "Even if it's Vietnamese," I thought, "Either way, I'm dead."

I ran across an open field, waving my arms. "Hey, wait, wait for me!"

As I got closer, I could see three American choppers, and my body flooded with relief. I didn't care that they pointed their rifles at me; I just kept running towards them.

As I got closer, they lowered their weapons. I made it to the nearest chopper, and the soldiers stared at me, frozen and wide-eyed, like I was a mirage. Only when I reached them did they realize I was an actual kid, with crapped-in pants and wearing an ear necklace, running through a jungle war zone.

One said, "What the hell are you doing here, kid?"

I shook my head, too breathless to speak, and they pulled me on board.

I lay panting on the floor as the chopper took off. The pilot kept turning his head around to look at me.

He said, "Who are you? You're just a little kid."

I shook my head and said, "I don't know."

He said, "Well, don't worry about it, okay? We'll find out who you are and your family, but you're one of us now, okay?"

We reached an army base, and the pilot took me to the commander's tent. I sat in a chair across from his desk, feeling numb with disbelief. Everything was a blur. The commander looked at me with narrowed, disbelieving eyes.

"Who are you?" He asked.

I was so scatterbrained I didn't know who I was.

I said, "I honestly don't know."

He shook his head and said, "Well, we'll get this figured out. Meanwhile, you need to get some clean clothes on and get rid of that necklace."

In my shocked state, I clutched the necklace defensively and shook my head. The commander said I could make a new necklace by collecting discarded peel tops from beer and soda cans that littered the base.

I was there for a few days. They gave me a uniform that didn't fit, so I used rubber bands to hold it down and walked around the base, picking up soda tops for my necklace. The guys there were all trying to figure out why I was there, who I came with, and how I got there.

After a few days, a government agent came to get me, someone I'd never seen before. I was flown back to the States and back to Bullhead City.

I had only been home a few weeks when my mother, Jackie, was murdered. We were sitting in the garage. As I worked changing tires, we talked about how we would move and start our lives over.

My mother said, "It won't be easy, but I really want to start a new life with you. We can do it. You can work in a garage, and we can make a living and do our own thing. We'll be our own little family."

She spoke with a glassy-eyed, faraway look that unsettled me despite the comforting and reassuring words. She was in a daze, and I could tell she was still recovering from a recent breakdown.

Then, she walked into the office area adjacent to the garage, and the next thing I knew, I heard shots: *Pop! Pop! Pop!* Racing outside, I saw her lying in a pool of blood, and I screamed and tried to run over to her. I wanted to gather her in my arms, but a government agent appeared out of nowhere, grabbed me by the arm, and pressed a gun to my head. Another agent came from behind, and they forced me into a station wagon, where I saw a little girl I had met the day before but couldn't recall who she was.

We drove to an office building that resembled a police station, and they brought me to a room with desks and a table. I was shocked and crying hysterically, but the two agents were oblivious. Seated at a table, they calmly discussed the profits from the murder, which involved stocks and shares in Kellogg and General Mills.

Then, one of them walked over and put a piece of paper in front of me.

He said, "This is a confession saying you killed your mother. I want you to sign it."

I shook my head, still crying, and screamed, "No, no!"

A dark-haired, muscular man in a suit barged into the office just then. He had a gun in one hand and a badge in the other.

He said, "I'm taking this kid."

He grabbed me and dragged me out of the building and into his car. We drove around for days. I never saw anyone so scared in my life. He kept driving in circles. My heart sank when we pulled up in front of the Quigley's. I stumbled out of the car, stared blearily at the house, and collapsed to my knees, burying my head in the dirt and throwing fistfuls of it over my head. Tears streamed down my face uncontrollably. It hit me like a ton of bricks—I had lost my entire family to murder, only to return to my step-family, who treated me like shit.

ADOLESCENT ESCAPADES

I have only scattered memories of the years immediately following 1975. I was enrolled in Yosemite High School but hardly ever went. I was always off doing other things. When school started, I didn't bother to go the first week, and when I did turn up, they wanted an excuse as to why I hadn't been there the first week, so I didn't go the next two weeks either. Over the years, I went to school on and off but never seriously.

During my time there, I mostly hung out at the picnic benches located on the hill, and other kids who were skipping class or just looking to relax would join. Despite Yosemite Lakes being known for all its crazy weirdness, it was also a chill community where teenagers could easily buy cigarettes, and those of us skipping class would gather to smoke and play happy-sack.

If there were a class I liked, such as a shop where we worked on cars, I'd go to school. There was also a history teacher I admired; we often discussed politics. One day, he took me aside and said, "I don't even know why I'm letting you go; you hardly attend school. But I'm just going to pass you along."

But when I attended math class after a long absence, the teacher said, "You don't show up here, and you're going to fail this class."

I stood to walk out and said, "I don't really need to come to your class."

Instead of attending school, I took on various odd jobs, doing anything to earn a buck. I loved to fix up old motorcycles and tear through the wind with my stereo blaring. I worked for two dollars an hour, restoring old Model A's and T's. I dug ditches, drove trucks, and worked in construction.

At one point, I was employed as a construction and maintenance worker in the gated community where we lived. My duties included sweeping gutters and filling in potholes. Later, I worked as a roofer, and eventually, I got a job in construction with Max Quigley's real estate partner, Armand, where I learned how to build a house from the ground up.

Armand had ten or twelve step-kids, and they all conspired on what happened next. One of the kids, Darren Price, invited me over. While hanging out, smoking pot, and drinking beer, Darren's brother, Donnie's girlfriend, mentioned, "I need a pack of cigarettes from the store."

I offered her a ride in my car, and she said casually, "Where's your gun at?"

In the back of my mind, I knew I was set up, but against my better judgment, I agreed to ride in her car instead of my own, where my gun lay hidden under the seat.

The mini-mart was only a few blocks away. Standing in line to pay, I felt a chill as a Mexican guy sidled up beside me, and another crept up from behind. Trying to keep my cool, I paid for my cigarettes, stepped outside onto the sidewalk facing the parking lot, and suddenly, one of the guys stepped in front of me, blocking my path. Craning my neck, I saw a few more guys coming towards us.

In a guttural whisper, the guy behind me said, "We're taking you out back to kill you."

I put my arm on his shoulder, gave him a big smile, and punched him in the mouth so hard his feet left the ground. Two guys grabbed me by the arms as he hit the ground, and another swung a crowbar into my stomach. Intense pain surged, but I was pumped with rage and adrenaline. There was a clash of fists, wrenches, and the crowbar, and I was beating them back.

Amid the chaos, I saw Donnie's girlfriend sitting in her car with the engine idling, watching me get beat up with glazed eyes like she was watching TV.

I screamed at her, "Just get the fuck out of here!"

It took her a second to come out of her daze and realize I was talking to her. Finally, she snapped out of it, and I ran to get in the passenger seat. Her tires squealed as we peeled out.

I hurt so bad after that, bruised and battered. But when I returned to work the next day, Max and Armand laughed at me. I was in so much pain that I couldn't even work, but they laughed.

Following everything that had happened, It seemed appropriate to wear my *Dead Kennedys* T-shirt whenever possible. That's what I was wearing one particular day when I was out on the boat dock at Yosemite Lakes.

Ted Kennedy and Maria Shriver showed up with a federal agent, who no doubt located me because of my chip. I don't know if these were real Kennedys or if they had already been replaced. After so much trauma, the line between reality and potential replacements gets blurred.

Maria got mad at me because of my shirt, saying it was disrespectful. I tried to explain that it was the name of a punk rock band that sings about social justice. Still, Ted dismissed my protests, saying I was a pothead and, therefore, he wouldn't bring me out into the public as the real John Kennedy Jr.

I think if he were any real family member, he would have died trying to get me out. If it were me, and I knew a family member was in trouble, I would die to help that person.

When I was seventeen, I had a girlfriend named Angela. We met at school and were seeing each other. I even tattooed her name on my arm. Then, one morning, when I was getting ready to go to school, Max stopped me and said, "You're not going to school today. You're getting on a plane and going to Canada."

So I threw some clothes in a bag and boarded a plane for Edmonton, Alberta, to stay with my sister, Debrah Quigley. Her husband, Jerry Van Dyke, was in the Secret Service, and his brother, John, was an awesome guitar player who had me writing songs. (Songwriting ability is a perk that comes from being in Mk-Ultra, and Max often used me for the same purpose.)

I'm sure Jerry knew about me when he asked me to write songs for him, but I was happy to do it anyway. I created lyrics like *Mama, I Want to Come Home,* and other songs. Jerry told me he knew somebody who wanted my music and would pay me. It turned out that the person was Ozzy Osbourne. Ozzy started singing my song *Crazy Train* and *Mama I'm Coming Home.* I wrote those songs, but I never got paid, and I never got credit.

I was in Edmonton for a year. The winter was long and cold, but since I was laid up after a bad motorcycle crash, I was okay with staying home and watching TV or playing Atari.

After I healed, I got a girlfriend who was twice my age. She had a Corvette and would sneak me into bars, even though I was underage. When it got warmer, I rode my skateboard all over the city, getting to know Edmonton. I kept calling and asking to come home, but Max and Dorothy said no, that I had to stay there a while longer. I never found out why, but something was going on.

When I finally came back to California, Angela had disappeared. I never saw her again. When Max saw the tattoo, he was furious. There couldn't be any distinguishing marks that would allow people to differentiate between me and John-John. So I removed it myself in my room, using a candle and an Exacto knife. I thought, welcome home. Welcome back to *Crazy Train*.

Max Jr. was completely insane. He tried to have me killed one time. We were driving around in his black Lincoln, visiting different friends of his. One of his friends was a federal agent who went by Steve as a civilian and Victor as an agent.

Victor was a screwball character who spoke about twenty languages and was a master of disguise. Once, he and Max Jr. took me through a shopping mall. We wound our way through a labyrinth of departments and hallways and ended up in a hidden room, an FBI office filled with desks and agents.

Victor once even swore me into the Secret Service. He recorded the whole thing on a reel-to-reel, which is out there somewhere. He also put a little tattoo on my side—just a series of little dots—and said, "That's the Little Dipper. If you ever end up dead, that's how we'll be able to identify the body."

But on this particular day, Victor tried to kill me, or at least pretended to. I hadn't seen him in a while. Max Jr. took me to his house, and he had long hair and was dressed like a hippy. That guy was a man of a thousand faces. When I first met him, he had a crewcut and looked like an FBI man, but he could look Mexican one day and white the next.

He had a young kid with him, maybe fifteen, and they got in the car with us. We drove for a while and wound up at the airport. I saw warehouses and a dumpster. We got out of the car, and I could hear the roar of the jets taking off and the whine as they landed.

By then, it was dark, and I was standing in front of the dumpster when the young kid and Victor pulled out guns. Victor was standing behind the kid, and he pointed a gun at my head. Max started rapping on the car's hood and shaking his head, nervous and jittery.

He said, "Hurry up and shoot this son of a bitch so we can get out of here."

Suddenly, a car pulled into the driveway across from us and beamed at us with its headlights. We lit up like we were under a spotlight.

Seeing it, Victor yelled at the kid, "No, don't shoot him."

The kid put his gun away and got in the car. The lights from the car across the way were still fixed on us, piercing through the darkness like a warden's eyes. Max got in the car, but Victor stood frozen behind the wood pallets. I walked over to him and told him I had a gun, which I did, tucked inside my belt.

I looked him in the eye and said, "I am going to win this battle, and you know it."

My head was spinning, and I didn't know what else to do, so I returned to the car. I thought, "I can't believe I'm getting back in the car with this crazy mother!"

The car took off, and the next thing I knew, we were pulling up to a nice brick house with white pillars on the porch. I looked around, wondering how the day could get any weirder. Where the hell were we now? We got out and went inside the house, and there, sitting on a tapestried armchair, was Betty Ford.

She said, "Hello, I'm Betty Ford."

I said, "It's nice to meet you."

And that was it! I returned to the car, combing my fingers through my hair, completely scattered and freaking out. By the time we returned to the Quigley's, it was three in the morning, and I came storming in.

I woke up Max and Dorothy and said, "There was just an attempt on my freaking life. What the hell is going on? I know you guys knew about it."

They said, "Well, you shouldn't have gone with your brother in the first place."

I don't know if that car showed up just in time to save me as a result of Wayne tracking me through my chip or if it was because Victor was really a double agent. All I know is that people have been watching over me and keeping me alive all these years.

SAN DIEGO NIGHTMARE

One day, the Quigleys introduced me to some new cousins from San Diego. I knew these cousins were connected to the disappearance or death of Opal May Edwards because I saw one of them driving around in her VW Beetle. He painted it so people wouldn't know, but I recognized the car.

When I met them, they said, "Come to San Diego. You can work in our auto paint shop. We'll pay you, and you can get back on your feet."

By that point, my life was such a mess, and with no better prospects, I agreed. Driving my pickup truck to San Diego, I soon discovered their financial troubles. They asked if I could sell my truck to help with their rent, and I reluctantly agreed.

After I started working for them, the situation went from bad to worse. Three attempts were made on my life. The first time, my cousin's boyfriend, a Navy man, came charging at me with a baseball bat, but I pulled out my .38 just in time, and he stopped and ran away.

Another incident happened in the garage when I noticed a stranger approaching.

"Look at the way that guy's walking, " I said to my cousin, easing my .38 out from under my belt. "He's definitely concealing a weapon. I hope I don't have to kill this guy in the street right now."

My cousin, seeing my gun, took off his hat and waved it up and down. The guy saw the signal, did a U-turn, and walked away.

The third attempt was more subtle and involved my older cousin. Fortunately, his son had warned me about his family's plans to kill me, so I was on the lookout. While I was working at the shop, his father came back from Taco Bell. He told me he had a Burrito Supreme for me in his office. Even though I was hungry, I wouldn't eat it because I thought it was probably poisoned. But he kept coming out to check on me.

"Come on, you gotta eat."

I said, "Really, man, I'm good."

At the end of the day, we returned to his office, where he had the food, and I saw the burrito sitting on his desk. He grabbed it and threw it against the wall, leaving a splatter of beans, rice, and a tortilla, which we watched slide down the wall before hitting the ground with a sad plunk.

He turned on me, eyes flashing with anger, and said, "My god-dam son!"

The final encounter occurred during a night at a local sports bar, where I was taken by one of my cousins. He was acting suspiciously, and I had a feeling someone would try and kill me again.

At the time, I was so broke I had to patch up my worn-out tennis shoes with duct tape. While playing pool, we talked with guys my cousin knew, and he introduced me to a slick-looking guy in a polo shirt.

My cousin said, "This is Scott. He's going to be our next boss."

After we left, my cousin acted oddly, avoiding my eyes and saying, "We have to wait here for somebody."

I knew what was coming, so I just turned around and walked away.

Years later, I recognized the Scott I met as the Scott Peterson who killed his wife. What's even crazier is that his girlfriend, Amber Frye, was the daughter of a guy I laid bricks for in Yosemite Park. That's how nuts that world is. Everyone's connected.

My stint at the auto paint shop only lasted for a few weeks, during which I slept in the garage, unpaid, with no money and no truck. They never paid me.

Finally, I went to their house where I'd left my suitcases and other possessions. But when I got there, the house was empty. They'd taken everything, including my suitcases. Now, I was stuck with no money, truck, or even a change of clothes. I called the Quigleys, and I was pissed.

I said, "You guys set this whole deal up. Now, my life is on the line. These guys tried to kill me. What's with all the attempts on my life? What the hell's going on?"

They evaded my questions and just sent me the money to come back home. From the horrors of homelessness to the home of horrors. I wished I could have afforded the luxury of flipping a coin.

HELL'S ANGELS

It was either Wayne or Wayne's father who first introduced me to the Hell's Angels when I was around five years old. He took me to a place where motorcycles were parked outside on a cement area littered with sharp, crushed stones. A guy tossed me a rag and showed me how to clean his motorbike, explaining how to get the water spots off the chrome.

Wayne knew the Hell's Angels could be trusted to keep me safe, so he brought me to their clubhouse in Fresnso in the early 70's, even before my mother was murdered. I started hanging out with them, but to me, they weren't just the Hell's Angels; they were brothers. Following my mother's murder, I earned my place as a patched member.

They put me through all sorts of tests and trials, and then they had the vote. We were sitting in the clubhouse in Oakland, California—Wayne was there—and everyone voted on whether I would be accepted into the family. They all voted yes, except for one holdout.

Wayne said, "Why are you holding out?"

With a smug grin, the guy said, "I'll tell you what: If you can get on your bike and get me a hamburger from Los Angeles, and it's still warm when you get here, you're in."

Wayne made a call, and a few hours later, a paper bag was delivered. He handed it to the holdout, and his green eyes widened like crosscut pickles when he saw the contents: atop stacks of hundred-dollar bills sat the requested hamburger and french fries. There had to be a hundred thousand dollars in that bag.

Standing there with a gun, Wayne said, "You're not touching that until the deal's done."

After that, I was in.

When it came time for my initiation, I entered the room, and all the Hell's Angels were lined up like rows of soldiers against the walls. Old Man John, a formidable figure, was at the podium.

He looked at me and said, "You're nothing but a piece of shit. You're nobody."

I shot back, "You know what? Fuck you! I'm John Kennedy, Godammit."

I was sure I was about to get the shit kicked out of me after that, but they let me walk out. Tears welled in my eyes because I thought I wouldn't get that patch on my back after all. Outside, I sat on the grass, feeling like crap. Then, one of the brothers came out and sat next to me.

"Are you really John Kennedy Jr.?" he asked.

"Yeah," I replied, avoiding his gaze.

He patted me on the back. "Well, I just want to let you know that you're in."

The day I received my patch was the greatest day of my life. But then, Sonny Barger, a founding member and a dear brother, delivered a bitter twist.

Asking for my patch back, he said, "You're a Hell's Angel. You'll always be a Hell's Angel, but we can't advertise you as one."

I was clueless about the strict hierarchy when riding with the group in the early days. The commander rides up front, and everyone follows in order of rank. We were on our way to Bass Lake, and, not knowing the protocol, I rode up front to greet Sonny.

I said, "Hey, Sonny! How are you doing, buddy?"

He glanced at me without smiling and fixed his eyes forward. Then, someone rode up alongside me and shouted, "Get your ass back where you belong."

I turned around and went to the back of the pack. When we reached Bass Lake, Wayne was there. The same guy who reprimanded me earlier laid into me again, "You can't just ride up to the front of the pack!"

Wayne shot him a look and said, "This kid can ride any fucking where he wants."

The attempts on my life continued. I have so many stories about being beaten up and almost killed. The Hell's Angels saved my life on more than one occasion.

We were sitting in the clubhouse once, and someone threw a hand grenade through the window to kill me. Dave was a brother who was sitting in a metal chair. The grenade blew up the chair, and we all stumbled outside to where we could see. He pulled his pants down, and one of the brothers started pulling shrapnel from his rear end and legs.

On another occasion, Wayne took me to a funeral for three Hell's Angels who were murdered. I don't know the whole story, and Wayne was so pissed off I didn't want to ask him, but he told me they died from saving my life. It's a terrible feeling to know that, just horrible.

The Hell's Angels have a strict code of secrecy, but there are a few anecdotes that I can share to illustrate what it was like to ride with them.

Long before I came along, The Rolling Stones hired the Hell's Angels for protection during one of their concerts. A guy rushed to the stage during the show, and the Angels pushed him back. After that, he tried again to climb on the stage with a revolver. One of the Angels, Alan Passaro, pulled a knife and stabbed the guy. Alan was arrested and charged with murder.

The Angels demanded Mick Jagger cover Alan's legal expenses, saying, "Hey, this Hell's Angel was there protecting you, and you should pay for his lawyer."

Mick Jagger refused. Years passed, and Alan was still in prison. So, the Angels decided to take matters into their own hands. We all got on a boat and headed to where Mick's yacht was anchored.

I didn't know the whole backstory and didn't realize that I was sitting on a case of dynamite in this little boat, headed to blow up Mick Jagger's yacht. All of a sudden, it started to rain, and it turned into a real downpour. We were all getting wet, and the dynamite was soaked.

In the end, we had to call it off and head back. After that, Wayne took me to see Mick Jagger, and I said, "Look, Mick, the Hell's Angels are going to kill you. Seriously, straight up! I was sitting on a case of dynamite that had your name on it. You need to pay them some lawyer money. That's all they're asking for."

Mick Jagger agreed and paid the lawyer fees. I don't know if he gave the money to Wayne and Wayne gave it to the clubhouse, but in the end, Alan was acquitted, and we didn't have to blow up Mick Jagger.

Once, a brother's motorcycle was stolen. We tracked it down, discovering it in this guy's garage where he was trying to paint and modify it so no one would know where he got it. We walked in, and the guy's face fell like a collapsed umbrella; he was visibly scared.

Sonny grabbed and forced him into a chair, telling me to hand him the power drill. I hesitated, confused, because the drill was right beside Sonny, and I didn't understand why he wanted me to come over and hand it to him.

"Get me the fucking drill!" He bellowed.

I quickly went over and got it for him. Sonny proceeded to jam it into the guy's foot, drilling it to the floor. Later, I realized why he wanted me to get it for him. With my fingerprints on the drill, the cops would be powerless. What could they say? That John Kennedy Jr., a Hell's Angel, had drilled a guy's foot into the floor? Considering that John-John was at Brown University then, it wouldn't have played out well.

The president of the Hell's Angels in Los Angeles went by the name "Big John." He was a big, burly guy with a military background and no sense of humor.

Once, while I was chatting with a girl at a bar, he approached from behind, pulled out his Bowie knife, and slashed my leather vest down the back, causing it to fall off. I stood there gaping at him in shock and disbelief. He would just do stuff like that.

Back then, it was a trend among young bikers to get a tattoo on their neck featuring a series of short dashes resembling a perforated line, accompanied by the words *cut here*. John often joked, "One of these days, I'm going to do it just for the fun of it." I kind of believed him.

For a time, I was staying at the home of a family I had met, sleeping on the couch. They treated me kindly, like family. However, when I went to Big John's house with Wayne, Big John casually mentioned, "By the way, I'm going to blow up the house where you stayed last night."

I said, "Dude, these people were kind enough to let me sleep on their couch. They took me in for the night, and you're going to blow them up? You're messed up, Dude. They have kids!"

He responded, "Put your money where your mouth is." I still don't know what he meant by that. Perhaps Jackie was paying him a lot, and he wanted more, or it was a test to see my reaction. Either way, a few of us went to this house. A brother brought a ladder, and we positioned it against the side of the house. Two brothers stayed on the ground, and one climbed onto the roof with me.

There was a rope going down the chimney. This guy instructed me, "Remember, Dave, hand over hand, pull this rope up."

Nervously, I pulled up the rope, hand over hand. We reached the bomb attached to the rope and pulled it up. It looked like a black shoebox with wires around the outside. Carefully, we went down the ladder, bomb in hand, and got into the car.

The device was sitting in the backseat between me and another guy. Everyone was silent. Suddenly, we hit a bump, and we thought we were done for. I saw myself getting evaporated in a fiery flash.

The bomb bounced in the backseat, but nothing happened. We didn't explode. Then we all busted up laughing. We couldn't believe we were still alive. Returning to Big John's house, it felt like some bizarre test. It wasn't a real bomb.

MARRIAGE MAYHEM

I was working in a donut shop in Fresno California, riding around on my motorbike with a blaring stereo. One day, I pulled into a local pizza parlor, where I met Lisa, a tall, attractive girl with shoulder-length blonde hair. We started talking, and then her father came to get her. He was a disgusting drunk, and I felt sorry for her.

Lisa and I started dating, and she once took me to her house. When we arrived, her father was beating the daylights out of her mother. She was lying on the floor unconscious, and he was kicking her and jumping on her. We grabbed her brothers and sisters, jumped in the car, and headed to the Quigleys. Lisa called the police, but the next day or the day after, they took me to a field in the country. Her dad pointed a shotgun at me and said, "If you ever call the police on me again, I'll kill you."

A short while after Lisa and I started dating, the Quigleys had an ice cream social. They got twenty pounds of ice cream and invited people over. A preacher was there, and his name was, funnily enough, Charlie Brown. He was a musician and had an album out. He also told me he was a gang member—I can't remember if it was the Crips or the Bloods—but he had a change of heart and became a preacher. During our conversation, he took me to his car, opened the trunk, and handed me a beautiful shotgun with a pot leaf engraved on the stock. It was a really cool gangster shotgun.

I said, "You're giving this to me? Wow, I can't believe you're doing that."

He said meaningfully, "You'll need it more than me."

Charlie Brown prayed for me at the ice cream social, laying his hands on my head, but it was a trick. When my eyes were closed, he chloroformed me. I was still semi-conscious as they picked me up and put me on the big island in the middle of the kitchen. Suddenly, I was floating above my body, looking down at myself and thinking, *Why are these people so mean?* I watched what they were doing with a detached concern.

They had taken my pants down and were operating on my testicles, performing a forced vasectomy. As I floated towards the bright light, thinking I would see God, I realized I still had some life to live. A sudden determination surged, and I floated back into my body. After that, I remember them dragging me roughly up the stairs to my bedroom.

When I woke up, I had no idea two weeks had passed. I had IV bags attached to my arms, and my testicles were in pain. I looked down and saw they were swollen and infected. In my groggy state, I ripped the IV needles out and ran downstairs.

When I saw Dorothy, I was confused and disoriented. I said, "Mom, I got an infection or something. I got grapefruits between my legs."

She got her purse, popped it open, and I saw she had syringes and all kinds of pill bottles, like a doctor. I thought, "That's so weird! What's she doing with all that stuff?"

She fished out a bottle of penicillin and thrust it at me. "Here, take one of these three times a day."

I looked at the brown plastic bottle, confused. I said, "Where's Charlie Brown?"

Max wandered into the living room and said, "Oh, he left while you were sleeping."

I ran up to his room, and sure enough, all his stuff was gone. A few days later, the phone rang, and I answered it.

"Where's Charlie?" A woman demanded. She sounded frantic.

I remembered Charlie had told me about a musical engagement he had scheduled for a few weeks after the ice cream social, and I said, "He told me he was going to a church event in another town."

I could hear her crying. She said, "Well, he never called me, and he never showed up. I want to know what happened to him."

I said, "Well, seriously, I have no idea. I haven't seen him. He's not here."

I hung up, and then I realized I probably wasn't the only one who died that night.

I was still in a drug-induced haze when the Quigleys said, "You're going to L.A. with Lisa."

Lost in a fog, I just did what they told me. We went to Lisa's grandparents' house outside Los Angeles in Norco, California, a modest, two-bedroom residential home. Lisa's grandmother and grandfather—who was deeply entrenched in military projects at Lear Sigler and connected to the mafia— hosted us for a couple of months. During that time, Lisa was obviously cheating on me, but I was too muddled to care.

One day, the grandparents said, "Come on, we're going to Las Vegas."

It was crazy. We got there in the middle of the night, pulling up into the parking lot of a cheesy Las Vegas wedding chapel. They rang the bell, and a man opened the door in his robe and pajamas.

The grandparents pushed us forward and said, "These two are here to get married."

The poor guy had to wake up his wife, the organ player, and Lisa's grandparents paid the extra ten bucks so we could have music.

I can't believe I did it. I can't believe I said, "I do." It was the corniest thing ever. I thought, "I'm John Kennedy Jr., and this is my wedding!"

We stayed one night at the Flamingo Hotel. That was our honeymoon. We went to see Red Foxx, and he called me out from the stage: "Why are you laughing so hard, you honky motherfucker?"

As soon as we got back, I found out Lisa was involved in a devil-worshipping cult with a guy named John Whitley, with whom

I'd attended grammar school. (His father was in one of those LSD cults and gave some to the two of us when we were just little kids.) Anyway, when I found out about that, I thought, "Why did I even get married in the first place?"

We were only married briefly, but it was a nightmare. When Lisa announced she was pregnant. I knew it couldn't be mine, but I went with it. I didn't make a fuss.

Then, when David was born in 1988, my brother Richard came to the hospital, and he was acting weird. He avoided talking to me like he thought he might be the father.

Just two weeks after David's birth, Lisa took David to Vermont to visit her friend Beth—the same Beth from the song by that name by the band Kiss. When she returned a few weeks later, it was with a different baby. We were at the Quigley's, and I freaked out.

I said, "What the hell? What's going on? This isn't my child. Why are you bringing back a different baby?"

Lisa wouldn't answer me, and I was getting increasingly upset.

Finally, Dorothy said to Max Jr., "Go take him for a car ride."

We drove somewhere, I don't remember where. I felt like I was in some crazy nightmare. We parked, and Max lit up a joint. I got high and was crying. I kept saying, "I can't believe she brought back a different baby!"

Max didn't say too much. They were clearly all in on this thing together and weren't telling me anything.

Back at the Quigley's, Beth's father called, and he was really upset. He wanted to speak with Lisa or Dorothoy, but they closed the door on me, and I don't know what was said after that.

I tried to go to the FBI, but they wouldn't help. Everyone told me that I was just delusional, so I took the baby home, and a few weeks later, when no one was there, I went to the Quigley's to search around and try and figure out what was happening.

That's when I found an extortion picture in Dorothy's room. It was a photograph of the new David perched on the lap of a guy named Robert Rogers, an old schoolmate. They sat on a low stone wall at the entrance to Yosemite National Park.

Robert, dressed in my clothes, also wore a clown nose and pointed a buck knife menacingly at David. I realized they were blackmailing the family in Vermont to whom the baby truly belonged. I pocketed that photograph and have it still.

A few months later, while playing with David in the front yard, he screamed in pain. Rushing to his side, I discovered a welt on his leg and a BB lying by his foot. Aware that John Whitley, involved in the cult with Lisa, owned a BB gun, I ran to his house to see if he was there.

His father's girlfriend answered the door and told me, "No, he's not here now, but he was acting real fucking weird. He came in, tossed his BB gun on the couch, and left."

Not long after that, someone tried to shoot me, only this time it wasn't a BB gun. I was working in the yard when a bullet came at me from out of the woods. It came so close to my cheek that I could smell the gunpowder. I ran to dive behind my car, and then I saw Lisa coming down the hill and shouted at her to get down.

After that, I tried going to the FBI again, this time in Fresno, California. When I got to the counter, I saw two guys in the back, and one said to the other: "Oh, it's David Quigley." They knew who I was before I got there and wouldn't talk to me.

I showed them the picture I found in Dorothy's room and told them a bullet almost got me. They said, "If they really wanted you dead, you'd be dead."

That may have been true, but they weren't done messing with me.

When Lisa was pregnant, I decided to fix up our property, and Lisa's grandfather offered a loan of five thousand dollars if I signed over to him the deed for the three acres I owned. I agreed and used the money to invest in a septic tank and gravel and make everything legal so I could buy a mobile home. It took a few years to get all the work done, and as soon as I did, he told me, "The property is mine, and I want you out of there."

Lisa's grandfather, Max Quigley, and a realtor named Breck Knott were business partners, and they stole the three acres from me. All three of them told me to go fuck myself. I spent night after night thinking about how I could kill them and get away with it, but in the end, I thought, "They'll get theirs eventually."

We moved into a small rental home, and Lisa convinced me to let Max Jr. come live with us for a while. Lisa was gone most of the time. She would go out to bars and see other guys. Even my brother Richard would pick her up and take her to the bar all night.

Max Jr. turned on a bunch of lights to grow pot in his room and turned up the heat so that I got a power bill for 500 dollars at the end of the month.

I said, "How am I going to pay this?"

It was all a setup to screw me over again. We'd only been in the house for two months and faced eviction because of the power bill. I was so broke I didn't even have enough for groceries. I was still working for Max and his partner, Armand, doing roofing and construction, and they were paying me next to nothing.

Little David and I went to the food bank one Christmas and got some green beans, dried onions, and rice-a-roni, which was our Christmas dinner. We were so hungry, and it tasted delicious. To this day, that was really one of the best Christmas dinners I've had.

David was about three years old, and I was sleeping on a mattress on the floor with David next to me. One night, I heard some whispering and a commotion behind me. I sat up, and Max Jr. had a gun pressed into David's hand and tried to coax him to pull the trigger. I jumped up and grabbed the gun out of his hand and said, "What the fuck are you doing?"

The next day, I took David outside and showed him what it felt like to shoot a gun. It scared the hell out of him, but I knew he would never touch that thing again.

I lost the rental due to the power bill, forcing me to sleep in my truck. I had no choice but to let David stay with the Quigleys since the truck wasn't suitable for a little kid.

One day at the community clubhouse, Dorothy appeared and handed me divorce papers, telling me they would seek custody of David since I couldn't provide him with a proper home.

Without money for legal representation, I reluctantly signed the papers. The entire situation had been designed to strip away everything, including my son. Lisa and her boyfriend purchased Max and Dorothy's six-bedroom home with the money they got from seizing my land and likely part of my inheritance from Opal May. Meanwhile, the Quigleys constructed a new house right next door.

I left Coarsegold after that and moved to Fresno to become a trucker. I drove all around the country for years, sometimes six or seven days a week. When I could, I rented an apartment in Fresno to be near David.

DANGER IN PENNSYLVANIA

I needed to get far away from the Quigleys. Over the years, I worked as a local truck driver, covering routes all around California. After that, I transitioned to long-haul driving, traveling from the East Coast to the West Coast. I also ran a truck driving school in Fresno, California, for about a year.

The school officials were happy with my training methods. I operated like a drill sergeant, but all my students got their trucking licenses, scoring on the tests in the mid to high nineties.

Then, wouldn't you know it, Max Quigley ended up working there. Things started to go south from that point on. I was dating a manager there, but she began telling stories about me and feeding the boss false information. On one occasion, I asked her if taking some students in a truck to Loughlin City to visit the casinos was okay.

I said, "We'll all take turns driving, and I'll teach them how to drive the highways."

She agreed and said it was a great idea, but once we were on the road, she told the boss I did it without permission, so he fired me.

That's how these setups worked. Everything that was done was to keep me broke and desperate. Who knows, Max Quigley could have owned that trucking company or just bribed the girl to lie about me.

I had hundreds of trucking jobs after that. I spent many birthdays and holidays in my truck or car, crying and wondering why the world was so fucked up.

I never kept a job for too long because I feared a hit. For instance, if the destination of a load changed suddenly or they sent me on a convoluted route with multiple stops, I'd know it was a setup, and I'd quit and search for another job.

Once, after I left a truck stop, my brakes wouldn't work, and I jackknifed on the road. I figured out who did it and confronted the guy, putting a gun to his head. But he pleaded with me, saying they had his wife and kids and would kill them if he didn't do as they said.

I let him go, but then he reported me for having a gun, so they fired me. But I always had a gun on me. I needed it. Even if I went swimming, I put my .38 in a plastic Ziplock bag and pinned it to the inside of my bathing suit.

I decided to move east to Pennsylvania. I had a girlfriend, Stacey, who convinced me to live with her in Mechanicsburg, where I could work for her family's trucking company. Wayne understood and said, "What do you need? I'll give you my Visa, Mastercard, American Express..." He was taking cards out of his wallet and flipping through them.

I said, "No, I can't take any money from you. You know that. I'm raised not to take any money."

He put his hand on my shoulder and said, "Good boy."

I drove to Pennsylvania and got an apartment. I had only been there a few weeks and was walking around a large outdoor flea market when I noticed a big black guy walking up and down the rows of tables. He was ringing a bell and talking about the end of the world.

Something was clicking in my mind, something Wayne had said about, "If you ever see someone ringing a bell..." But I didn't have time to finish my recollection because I caught sight of Wayne at one of the tables. He gave me a quick nod as if to say, "Keep walking," a sign that he didn't want to talk to me.

I walked on and, at a table nearby, noticed an urn I recognized from childhood. When I picked it up, I couldn't believe what I'd found: It looked exactly like an urn that had belonged to Aristotle Onassis and contained his grandmother's ashes. He had me clean that urn several times, and I knew what it looked like inside.

So I opened the lid and saw it had the same engravings, and I knew it was the same one. I'm sure it was planted there by Wayne for me to find. It's something he's done several times in my life. I bought it, so I have that one keepsake from when Aristotle was in my life.

Carlisle turned out to be another mafia-run town, and the whole situation was another setup. I was living with Stacey and working for Carlisle Carriers, driving Heinz products all over the country. One night, returning home exhausted after unloading a truck from New Jersey, I went straight to bed, oblivious to any danger.

Suddenly, I felt a crack in the back of my head, jolting me awake. There, standing with a gun pointed at me, was Stacey, cocking the weapon as if getting ready to shoot. I knocked the gun from her hand, and it clattered to the floor. Moving quickly, I tried to reach it before she could, but she was scrambling for it, so I punched her in the leg and threw her on the bed.

Grabbing the gun, I shoved it in my pants and, feeling totally confused and freaked out, hastily gathered some things and ran out of the house. Before I got too far, I saw headlights coming at me and caught a glimpse of Stacey's face before she tried to run me over. I couldn't believe what was happening. I cut across some residential properties and a field and reached a motel, where I got a room.

The next thing I knew, I heard pounding on the door. When I opened it, a hundred cops pointed their guns at me. I honestly think I peed my pants at that point. I was completely overwhelmed.

They grabbed me, and I said, "What the hell is going on?"

No one answered. They shoved me in the back of a police car and took me to jail. A week passed, and no one even let me have my phone call. When I finally got in front of a judge, I could have sworn she was my old Yosemite Lakes High School principal—either that or her identical twin.

I said, "Can I tell you my side of the story?"

She said, "No, I don't want to talk to you. I heard her side, and that's enough for me."

She wouldn't let me say anything. I tried to talk to the cops who were taking me to jail after I saw the judge.

I said, "You know, I've been on the right side of the law for way too long for this shit to be going on."

But they just threw me in jail and wouldn't let me use the telephone or speak to a lawyer. I was sure someone was going to come and kill me, and they'd just find me there, dead. Finally, Max sent me money for a lawyer. The lawyer knew who I was, the real John Kennedy Jr., and somehow, he got all the charges dismissed, wiping my arrest record clean.

In the end, I realized the whole thing was a plot to get me whacked. Stacey's boyfriend was one of the cops. She was trying to get him to kill me by saying I abused her, but she was mafia.

After Stacey, I joined another trucking company, handling maintenance and forklift operations. It was owned by my new girlfriend, Renée's family. They ran all kinds of scams, including ripping off the US Army by repacking the contents of the pallets to get two or three loads into one truck.

Wayne reappeared, taking me to Atlantic City on weekends. I think he had it in his head from way back that I'd come out one day. Once people knew who I was, he wanted me to run the place.

Wayne arranged for Renée and me to stay at different hotels so I could walk around and get to know the town. After a while, the hotel owners started giving me free rooms. Despite the free accommodation, I only made ten dollars an hour and didn't have the money to go one weekend.

I asked my boss for a raise. I said, "Look, you guys are only paying me ten dollars an hour, and I'm basically running the place. You can pay me a little bit more than that."

They wouldn't do it, so I explained, "It's because I want to go to Atlantic City again this weekend, but I don't have the money."

I guess those were the magic words because my boss kept giving me side work over the next four days. Trucks would show up, and the drivers would get out and tell me, "Hey, I need this little thing moved from here to there." Then they'd give me 200 dollars. By the end of the week, I had 1,200 dollars to go to Atlantic City. Then, the next week, those same people tried to kill me.

A guy named Edwards appeared and started being a real prick to me. I remembered the name in connection to Opal May and didn't think much of it at first. But he must have made a deal with Renée's family.

One day, not long after he left, I was loading a truck, using the forklift, and then Gary, one of the brothers who worked in the warehouse, must have signaled to Ron, Renée's other brother who was in the control booth. He got on the radio and told the truck driver it was okay for him to leave while I was still loading. I flew off the forklift and cracked my head on the side of the jitney.

I knew I had to move on after that. Somebody bribed the family, and they wouldn't stop at one failed attempt on my life.

I didn't know where to go, but the whole time I was in Pennsylvania, the Quigleys had been writing to me, saying things like, *please come back. We want you to be a part of our family again.* After the forklift incident, Max sent me 5,000 dollars to pay for my move back to California.

I took the money and bought a used moving truck, putting in some extra work to get it up and running. That way, I'd have my own vehicle instead of renting one when I returned to California. Unfortunately, it became clear that the Quigleys weren't interested in helping me get back on my feet—they wanted me broke and jobless.

First, Renée and I found ourselves a home in Raymond, California—a tiny town with only a single grocery store and two bars, located 20 miles from the nearest civilization. Soon after, Max arrived out of the blue, demanding I pay back the money he'd lent me. I had to sell the truck, leaving me stranded without a car or a job in the middle of nowhere. I was all messed up again.

Renée's sister showed up one day, and I heard her screaming hysterically, "You're not my sister! You're not Renée! What did you do with my sister?"

So Renée was another fake, another put-up job. I couldn't believe it.

The Quigleys sometimes stopped by with leftovers, but I always tossed them out because they could be poisoned. One day, Max came around with a plate of cookies. We went for a drive, and he bit into one and seemed fine, so I ate a few and then developed an excruciating stomach ache. I told Max I thought the cookies were poisoned, and he took the plate and tossed it out the car window as if he knew Dorothy would try and get me sick.

I got a job as a truck driver and was away for about a month. When I got back, I called Renée from the truck stop to come and get me, but she refused. She said she already found a boyfriend—I later found out he was about sixteen years old—so I had to sleep in the truck.

I wound up letting Renée have the house. She later became good friends with the Quigleys, and they hired her to work for them. The Quigleys loved to torment me by bonding with women who had betrayed me. That was the worst move I could have made: returning to California.

BATTLEFIELDS AND BLACK OPS

Wayne wanted me to learn about every military branch, taking me for training all over the country. He explained, "You're doing this for your family. You're getting trained, and you'll get revenge on your family."

I'd show up at different places for basic training, but no one told me anything; I was just told to shut up.

Once, during Navy training, I was underwater, and a guy pulled a knife and tried to stab me. I came up too fast, trying to escape him, and got the bends.

Pulling off my oxygen mask, I yelled, "This motherfucker just tried to kill me with his knife. What the hell is going on?"

They responded that I shouldn't have come up so fast.

I looked at them in disbelief and said, "Well, what would you do if a guy had a big knife and was going to kill you?"

They didn't say anything and just threw me in this big metal pressurized tank for two or three days. I thought I would go crazy in that thing.

In army basic training, I was told to pack heavy mortar shells. The officer instructed me to bang the tube on my leg after loading, but I refused.

I said, "If I bang it on my leg, I'm going to blow my leg off, if not worse."

Wayne showed up just then, and the officer and another guy he was with started running in the other direction. I turned the mortar on them, wanting to blow them up just for the hell of it, but Wayne said no.

"You let me do the killing."

Everything I did with the military was hush-hush, all black ops, doing stuff you're not supposed to do for the government. It's never official in black ops, and I never got paid.

Once, when I was "under," Wayne took me to the White House. There were shoe-box-sized boxes on a shelf in a room with computers and file cabinets. Wayne opened one and showed me all the paychecks made out to David Keith Quigley. If those paychecks are still around, I want my money!

Another time, Wayne took me to an airport in Cambodia with a military plane painted all black. It had a 50-caliber rifle on the door, but it was such a top-secret mission that when the gun fired, the shells couldn't go outside like usual; they just fell inside the chopper. At the end of the mission, I had to pick up all the shells off the floor and stash them in a bucket because they didn't want anyone finding American-made shells lying around Cambodia, blowing our cover.

River Escape: A Cambodia Rescue Mission

Officially, America wasn't supposed to be in Cambodia, so everything we did there was black ops. I was sent there with a unit to rescue some POWs captured after their spy plane crashed.

Our helicopter touched down, and I recall landing in the jungle with a heavy pack on. We were two days away from a POW camp along the river and had to hike in. I was packing so much that I had blisters on my feet, making walking hard. Using some dry straw, I stuffed it into my boots to absorb the moisture from my oozing sores.

Finally, we reached the top of a hill overlooking our destination: a river and a small village below. When we got to the river, I was instructed to get in the water and float down. Even though my mission was explained, I screwed up and got caught.

I lowered myself into the river and started floating towards the camp. The water was a cool relief, and the burbling noise made it easy to disguise any sound I might inadvertently make. I was happy to let the current do the work for a change, trying to stay as low in the water as possible.

As I floated, I felt myself going too fast. Reaching for some bamboo to my right, I missed it and ended up putting my hand on a dock to slow down. That's when a gun was pressed to my head, and two Vietnamese guys in large, floppy straw hats grabbed me, pulling me onto a wooden pier and dragging me 20 feet down where some four-by-four bamboo cages floated in the water.

They were yelling at me, but I couldn't understand anything other than the ferocious anger in their voices. Then, they shoved me into one of the bamboo cages, placed in a way that prevented me from touching the bottom. I cried out in pain as bamboo spikes pierced my back. There were captured soldiers in cages on either side. I couldn't see the soldier to my left but heard him crying in pain. A Vietnamese soldier approached him, put a gun to his head, and shot him. The water turned red with his blood, and I completely lost it, crying.

The soldier to my right said, "You better shut up, or you'll be next."

So I stuck my head underwater to muffle my cries, bubbles escaping like air from a submerged soda bottle.

Then, a man from the pier stuck his rifle through the bars of my cage and pointed it at my head, screaming at me. I thought my days were over, and I squeezed my eyes shut, praying and thinking I wasn't ready to die. The soldier to my right said he didn't think he would make it much longer. I told him to swim towards me and put my arms through the bamboo and under his to keep him afloat. I kept whispering, "They'll come for us, they'll come for us. Just stay alive." Hours passed, but he never responded.

Night fell. My arms and body were numb, and I was going into shock. Suddenly, the village erupted with artillery fire. The boat dock was hit, and I was blown through the water and out of the cell. I remember somebody grabbing me by the shirt and hauling me to the shore. As they pulled me along, someone yelled, "We weren't ever here!"

I think I was half dead from the explosion, and I don't remember much after that—just lying in a stretcher in the mud with someone working on me. My ears rang, and I shouted as I asked the medic if the other guy had made it, but he just shook his head; no.

I believe I came to in the hospital ward of an aircraft carrier. After I woke up, they kept me under lock and key, like I was their top secret project.

Jonestown: Jungle Justice

Wayne took me to a military base, probably Guantanamo, in my late teens. No one else was there when I arrived. My job was to put sheets on all twenty of the beds in the barracks. After that, I was handed a jump rope and told to skip rope to keep exercising.

Finally, some guys in military gear showed up, and I asked, "Where am I? What am I doing?"

They said, "You're in the military. Shut the fuck up. Don't ask no questions. It's none of your business."

When we got in the chopper, they made sure we didn't have anything in our pockets. That was routine with black ops. You couldn't have any personal possessions like rings or watches, and they would never tell us where we were going or how we were getting there.

When we landed in the jungle of Guyana, I saw all the dead bodies. They were everywhere: on the ground underneath an open pavilion and all around the outside. I just froze for a minute in a state of suspended animation. Then someone shouted at me to start loading the bodies in the tin cans, military speak for cheap coffins.

Around the outside of this crazy compound with speakers hooked up to the rafters, they had some picnic tables. We put the bodies on the table, and some guys were there in lab coats to identify the bodies before we loaded them in the cans.

Wayne was arguing with the cult leader, Jim Jones, inside the compound. He wouldn't drink the cyanide-laced Kool-Aid he'd made his followers swallow, so Wayne pulled out a pistol and pointed it at his head.

He said, "You're going to die with the rest of these motherfuckers."

And he did. Wayne shot him.

But the whole massacre was pre-planned. It was payback because the cult followers killed a senator who came down from California. He might have been there to collect money, and they shot him instead of paying him. The senator was probably a connected guy because the order came down from the top after that: Kill every single one of them.

Obamas

I was in my twenties when Wayne took me to Hawaii. We talked about Obama, and Wayne said, "I think we'll just have to make him president."

I don't know if what follows was staged, but we were in a nice house with big double doors leading to a specific bedroom. Wayne told me that Obama was sleeping inside, and my job was to spend the night guarding the entrance to the bedroom. He told me I wasn't to sleep but lie there and protect Obama with my life, if necessary. Sure enough, two men wielding AK-47s appeared through a separate doorway and opened fire, but I shot them both dead.

That wasn't my only encounter with the Obamas in the early days, and I don't know if this was a setup, but I met Michelle Obama in a bar in Fresno when she was a college student. We had drinks and wound up in my apartment. Anyway, I can't comment on who or what Michelle Obama is today—maybe a body double, I don't know—but the Michelle Obama I met then was most definitely a woman.

When Johnny Comes Marching Home

I can't remember what mission ended in a helicopter crash that left me in traction at Walter Reed Hospital. All I remember is the pilot saying, "We're going to crash."

We hit the ground two seconds later, and my ass went through my chin. I was in a metal rack at the hospital and couldn't move my body. It was hell for weeks. I was so itchy, but I couldn't scratch.

It was summertime, close to the Fourth of July, when Dolly Parton arrived at the base to put on a show for the holiday. She entered my room and told me she wanted me at the performance. They planned to bring me down from the hospital to a place on the lawn so I could watch the show.

On the night of the show, I came to the spot she'd told me about and lay on a blanket on the grass. I couldn't believe I was there. I felt half dead. But then she started singing "When Johnny Comes Marching Home," I could tell she was nervous and even messed up her lines.

I knew it was for me. That's why she came to my room. I had to lie splayed out on a blanket in the grass in a body cast during the heat of summer to watch Dolly Parton marching in place in a red, white, and blue body suit with little white boots just to be taunted.

When I watched the video of that performance, I saw the camera pan over to a military commander in the audience and stay on him. Later, as I lay in bed in that hospital week after week, I realized he had set up the whole situation that caused the crash.

Arizona Train Derailment

In 1995, I was working as a truck driving instructor when I felt an urge to share my story. However, I struggled to write due to past torture that affected my ability to make coherent notes. When I attempted to write, the words were barely legible and made no sense when I tried to read them. So, I decided to record my memories instead. Whenever I could, be it while driving or having a break, I would use a tape recorder to document my memories of everything that happened.

While instructing a newcomer named Rick James, we heard over the radio that a train had derailed in Palo Verde, Arizona, resulting in one death and multiple serious injuries. It was ruled as sabotage, and a note left by the terrorist said it was payback for the events in Waco, Texas, where cult members were burned alive by the FBI. President Bush offered a 325,000 dollar reward for information leading to the terrorist's capture.

Because of my military and Black Ops background, I could tell Rick James was Special Forces, but I considered him a good guy. He once said, "You know, Dave, I've met a lot of people in my life, and you're one of the best they've got. You are absolutely one of the best they've got."

During a break in the desert, we both got out to walk around and stretch our legs. Rick went one way, and I went another. When we returned to the truck, we started talking again, and he admitted his Special Forces background. We discussed our military experiences, and eventually, Rick James confessed to orchestrating the train derailment, explaining how he rigged a wire from one track to the next to prevent detection.

I did my best to stifle the seismic jolt that went through me when he said that and fixed my eyes on the road, nodding with affected sympathy and muttering some platitudes. But after I dropped him off in Bakersfield, California, I reported it to the FBI.

I said, "Hey, I just trained a guy who's a terrorist, and he did the Arizona Amtrak derailment." But they didn't do anything, not then and not anytime since.

Upon returning to my truck, I discovered my tapes were missing. The whole business of Rick being in my truck was a setup to prevent me from sharing my story. Frustrated and upset, I recalled some details Rick shared about his childhood, realizing he felt oddly familiar, almost like a relative. Someone knew I was making those tape recordings and stole them.

SURVIVAL, REDEMPTION, AND RESCUE

Things were going okay in 2012. My girlfriend and I had a trailer on a friend's property in Coarsegold, California, but mostly, I lived in the back of a novelty store that I owned called "The Magic Mojo." It was a great little place, and I loved running it. In town, people called me "The Mojo Man." I used to get up at five in the morning, mop the floors, and set everything up. It was a labor of love.

Because it was right next to a McDonald's drive-through, lots of people stopped by after getting their food. We sold all kinds of antiques and novelty items that we picked up from flea markets and estate sales and sold artwork that I painted. There was a section for jewelry, kitchenware, toys, books, you name it. Outside was a box for food donations, where homeless people could come by and grab something to eat.

They could have left me alone. I would have been happy. I wasn't asking anyone for anything or even thinking of coming out at that time. But as I said, I do believe the Satanic circles that control our current reality and have some future-looking technology, possibly Project Looking Glass or something similar: a recovered relic of ancient technology that generates images of what the future could look like, based on current events. And I think their forecasts involved me coming out and ruining their plans for a New World Order under the fake Donald Trump and a resurrected fake John Kennedy Jr.

I got sick. I think it was poisoning. I had terrible acid reflux, and when I went to the doctor, he diagnosed it as a hiatal hernia requiring minor surgery with three small incisions on my stomach and a few days in the hospital.

However, when I woke up from the surgery, I had six incisions on my abdomen and was in terrible pain. They dragged me around the hospital for X-rays, which showed three holes in my lungs and organs.

They kept me there for ten days and totally abused me. It was a living hell. I was screaming for pain medicine, but they wouldn't give it to me. At one point, I was dying, and they had to bring me back using defibrillators that left burn marks on my chest and caused me to buck so violently on the table that I suffered permanent injury to my back.

After ten days, I managed to pull myself into the bathroom, shave, and clean up before checking myself out. They tried to keep me there, but I told them, "You guys are trying to kill me."

I got a ride back to the Quigleys, but after one night, Max said, "You're not welcome here."

So I got another ride back to my trailer, but it had been emptied out. My girlfriend stole my truck and all the merchandise we'd bought and stored in the trailer. Everything was gone.

The landlady for The Magic Mojo wanted me to stay, but without a truck and with all my merchandise stolen, I knew there was no way to keep the place going. All I had left was my trailer and my son.

I tried to get a disability allowance after they messed me up so badly in the hospital. I got a lawyer, but someone must have paid him off. Initially, he didn't show up to the court hearing, so it had to be rescheduled. When he did show up, I had tears streaming down my face, and he taunted me, saying, "You little pussy! What are you crying for?"

"Oh, so they paid you off, too!" I shouted.

At the end of the hearing, the judge granted my disability. She said, "You can't work." But then, when the letter arrived, it said my disability had been denied.

My lawyer became unreachable after that, and I knew I'd been scammed again. I lost everything. The government was so desperate to keep me in poverty, so I could never tell my story that they even cheated me out of my disability.

David was in a bad way. I think the Quigleys had been poisoning him and torturing him. He would sit and stare at the computer screen all day. Once I was strong enough, I visited him and knew it was time to go. I showed him some pictures of Bullhead City and said, "Look, we can get out of here. We can find a house real cheap in Bullhead."

We looked through real estate listings and saw a house for sale for 9,000 dollars.

David said, "Dad, let's buy that one."

So we got in my camper and drove to Bullhead City. Unfortunately, the house we wanted had sold by the time we got there, and we wound up camping by the river for a few months until we found a new place for sale. The asking price was 15 thousand, but I bargained them down to 12 thousand cash.

We moved in and fixed the place up, and David and I have been living here ever since. I have a motorbike that I fixed up and ride down to the river sometimes. I remember my mother and Aristotle. They were both murdered and buried here. I believe I know where they put my mother: a dirt-filled area encircled by a chain with a flagpole and anchor in the middle. I'm glad I can be close to her. David is getting better. I love him with all my heart and take care of him the best that I can.

Most mornings, I go to church and see my friends. They give out free loaves of bread, and I go to the thrift store or the food bank to get food.

I haven't heard from Wayne in years. I wish I knew what happened to him. I have so many questions I want to ask him.

I've had no income since 2008, and today, I suffer from diabetes, heart failure, COPD, arthritis, and nerve damage. But once, a long time ago, I was a little boy beat up and locked in a dog cage. I told myself then and tell myself now, "Out of the darkness and into the light."

About five years ago, I got a free government phone, so I had a means of making videos for Facebook and Twitter. After I got the letter denying my disability, I was giving Brenda a ride in my car. That's when AC/DC's *Hail Caesar* came on the radio. I started singing along, and she realized with surprise that it was me on the album. We both laughed, and then I was quiet for a moment.

I said, "You know, I think I'm ready to tell my story."

She said, "Why? Are you crazy? Why would you want to start all that shit in your life again? Things are okay now. Why don't you just leave it alone?"

Because I can't. I must tell my story. Some people have done everything to kill and silence me; others have risked and even given their lives to keep me safe. I don't know how long I have to live, but you need to know the truth before I die.

TRUST THE PLAN?

I n 2017, I started sharing my story on Facebook and Twitter, but my account got blocked and hacked. I kept making videos, but no one was seeing them. Then, in 2023, I started sharing on TikTok, and suddenly, people started to find me. The relief, joy, and optimism I felt after I found people who were finally ready to hear my story and believe me was indescribable, and I'm so grateful!

At the same time, I got a lot of hate in the comment section, and at first, I thought it was just typical government trolls trying to discredit me. Then some of my supporters told me about 'Q' and how a whole segment of society—the very same demographic who could otherwise be counted on to gather their forces and fight against an evil government—were sitting on their hands and waiting for Donald Trump and John Kennedy Jr. to save them. My God!

Then, I knew why God saved me for this moment. I understood why Wayne made a point of having me witness certain events: Reagan dismissing the idea of a wall, Donald Trump's death, John-John's death, and even, possibly, those aliens in the coffins in a bunker under New York. Because I think that is all meant to play into this doomed and demented endgame we're all participating in.

Earlier, I referred to the Russian connection. When Stalin was coming to power, he organized his takeover in five-year plans, the first of which was called "Operation Trust." The point of this operation was to convince people loyal to the old regime that they shouldn't worry. Within the government and military, anti-Bolshevik operatives had infiltrated at the highest levels and secretly worked to subvert the communist revolution. Citizens who were loyal to the old royal order need not fear. A plan was in place. "Just trust the plan," they were told. So they did.

AFTERWORD

I want to express my heartfelt thanks to all those who have supported me in sharing my story on social media and those who have sent me cards, gifts, and words of encouragement. There are so many of you that I can't mention everyone individually. Your support means everything to me, and I am endlessly grateful. Please continue to help spread my story and uphold the truth by leaving a review for this book. Thank you, and may God bless each and every one of you!

Warm Regards,

John

ABOUT THE AUTHOR

John F. Kennedy Jr., the son of the late U.S. President John F. Kennedy, experienced a dramatic turn of events at nine when he was substituted by a body double. The replacement, who died in a plane crash in 1999, led a life of affluence and privilege. Meanwhile, the real JFK Jr. entered the witness protection program and endured a life marked by torment, mistreatment, and MK-Ultra programming. He currently resides in Bullhead City, Arizona.

Jackie Goldman is an author and ghostwriter living in Brooklyn, New York. You can visit her online at: www.JackieGoldman.com

Credits:

Printed in Great Britain
by Amazon

46081035R00099